Home Beermaking

Home Beermaking

Brian Leverett

Prism Press

Published in 1980 by

PRISM PRESS
Stable Court
Chalmington
Dorchester
Dorset DT2 0HB

ISBN Hardback 0 907061 07 9
ISBN Paperback 0 907061 08 7

Printed and Bound in Great Britain
by Purnell and Sons (Book Production) Ltd.,
Paulton, Bristol

Author's Foreword

It is as easy to brew beer as to make a cup of coffee although there are a few more stages to it. Unfortunately it took me ten years to realise this!

My own brewing experience dates back to the early sixties, when ingredients were more difficult to obtain than they are today and background information was almost non-existent. As a result, my early attempts produced a beer that was almost undrinkable, I say *almost*, as I drank it rather than lose face—like so many home brewers before I would nip down to the pub on the slightest excuse, rather than swallow my own beer.

Gradually, new equipment and ingredients became available, and it was no longer necessary to spend the whole day making the brew or to have every room in the house smelling like a brewery. Above all, the standard of the beer was far higher.

Today, there are basically five different methods of brewing beer, and both the beginner and even the experienced brewer may be uncertain about which method is the best, and also about the part played by the various ingredients used in the brewing process.

The aims of this book are threefold: to consider the relative merits of each method; to provide simple, easy-to-follow instructions for them and to give sufficient background knowledge for the home brewer to understand the processes and adapt them to his own purposes.

Even though homebrewing has become so simple that anyone can do it, it is still a skill. It is doubtful whether any truly worthwhile skill can be learnt entirely from a book, but I hope that as a result of reading this you will be satisfied with your very first brew, and that through experimentation along the lines suggested, you will be able to make your own distinctive beers in any style you choose.

The choice is yours. I have outlined the advantages and disadvantages of each method as I see them. I myself usually make my beers from kits, in the same way that I use instant coffee rather than coffee beans. Other people prefer to make their beers by the longer mashing method. Someone told me recently that they had started mashing because they found it more worthwhile and satisfying than simply opening a tin. Personally, I get my pleasure from drinking beer, rather than from making it. But many people do get immense satisfaction from brewing, and I have explained how you can make your beer by the traditional method.

It would be wrong to think that the idea of

home brewing is new. Brewing originated in the home, and up until fairly recent times the farmer's wife would brew large quantities of ale, which were given to the workers at the end of the day as part of their wages. Beer has for centuries been part of many people's staple diet. The revival of interest in home brewing is just another example of the modern desire to return to a simpler, more natural life.

I am all for the preservation of traditional methods which have evolved over the years. Brewing methods are continually changing: hops were introduced; better quality barleys were used; the significance of brewing water was recognised and specialised yeasts and isinglass were developed. All these contributed to the continually-changing process. Malt extracts, heading liquids, new equipment, are all helping to change the methods further to produce tomorrow's traditional techniques.

I have adopted the principle used in my previous books and retained what I consider to be the best of the old methods, as well as including new ingredients and equipment where they improve the quality of the beer and make our task easier. Nothing has been excluded simply because it is old. Nothing has been included just because it is new, unless it represents a worthwhile improvement.

There are a number of excellent pieces of equipment on the market, and I have mentioned by name only those which I have personally used. Due to differences in taste there is little point in recommending specific brands of malt extract or beer kits. In general I have found little to complain about with any of the beer kits sold–this is a very competitive market and standards are high—and would certainly recommend you to try some as an introduction to home brewing.

Brian Leverett
Poole
Dorset
1980

CONTENTS

Acknowledgements

I should like to thank the following people who have provided me with background information on their products: Mr. R. Pritchard of E.D.M.E., Mr. N. Instone of Southern Vineyards, Mr. H. Ritchie of Ritchie Products, Welbeck Advertising. I would also like to acknowledge literature sent to me by various firms in connection with features I have written.

I should like to thank my many homebrewing friends at the Poole Wine Circle, too numerous to mention, for many long discussions on homebrewing methods.

I would also like to thank Colin Browning for his artistic interpretation of my manuscript and the staff of Prism Press for the conversion of this manuscript into a book.

Chapter 1

Introduction

It is estimated that over two million people make their own beer in the United Kingdom, and this is only a fraction of the world total.

The most obvious reason for the popularity of home brewing is the tremendous savings that can be achieved by making, rather than buying, beer. The magnitude of these savings are seldom realised, even by those who practise the art. By brewing his own beer, a man who drinks two pints a day and who earns the national average wage can (according to the type of beer he drinks and where he buys it) save up to 10% of his disposable income. Of all the methods of self sufficiency designed to save money, few are easier and more effective than homebrewing.

Unfortunately, many who start to make their own ales and stouts are disappointed to find that the resulting drink is a frothy, bitter, yeast flavoured liquid that is extremely high in alcohol. On seeking advice the would-be brewer is often told that to make a good beer it is necessary to mash. This, it is suggested, requires expensive equipment, the expertise of a chemistry graduate, and all the time in the world.

This is a book written for ordinary people who want to make a top quality beer, designed to suit their palate, cheaply, with the minimum amount of effort and without dedicating their lives to the pastime.

Since home brewing restrictions were lifted in Britain in 1963, the hobby has become extremely popular and an industry has grown up to cater for its needs. As a result, it is now possible to buy ingredients in a semi-prepared form with most of the more difficult and time-consuming operations already performed by professionals using the best equipment. This has led to new and easier methods of making beer.

The beginner is often confused as to which method is best for his purpose. All the methods have advantages and disadvantages, and you will have to make up your own mind. I have tried to discuss these methods and given my personal views where appropriate, but not everyone will agree with them. I have also included a fairly comprehensive range of recipes. Obviously, it is impossible to formulate recipes to every individual's taste, so the full theory of compounding recipes has been included. Anyone who is not satisfied with their beer can adjust it to suit their own preferences. Personal choice and simplicity are the central themes of this book. The theory and practice of home brewing is simple, and once you know and understand it you will no longer be at the mercy of people who insist on telling you how to make your beers. You will no longer wonder whether you are using the best methods and ingredients, but above all, no one will be able to dictate the brand of beer you drink or the price you pay for it.

Most people start by trying to make the kind of beer they usually buy in the pub. After the first few pints they realise that theirs is a different type of beer—full-bodied, in which the yeast is alive. Just a few pints are usually enough to convert them to home brews for life, and they soon abandon all attempts to copy what they were drinking before. Comparing home brewed ales with those that you buy is like comparing a loaf straight from the oven with a sliced wrapped loaf. I know which I prefer!

Legal Position

In Britain it is legal to brew as much beer as you wish for your own and your friends' consumption. Readers in other countries should check with the authorities if in doubt. But it is illegal to sell beer without a special licence in Britain, and details of the licence can be obtained from the Customs and Excise. Raffling, or disposing of it in any way for gain is forbidden, even if the money goes to charity.

It is a serious offence in many countries to drive with alcohol in the blood above a certain level. This level will often be reached after drinking far smaller volumes of home-made beers, which are usually stronger than their commercial equivalents.

Equipment

Unlike most hobbies very little expense is involved when you begin. Until you have finally decided how you intend making your beer, and how much you will be drinking, it is advisable to buy only the essentials. There is a whole range of items available to the brewer which make his task easier. While some of these are extremely useful, they are by no means essential. As your knowledge and interest increases you may wish to add to your equipment, but until that time comes you should be able to adapt the apparatus you already possess. What you do buy will last for several years, so it is better to invest a little more and buy only the best. If you already make wines you will possess most of the basic apparatus: if not you should be able to improvise with items from the kitchen.

You will need a white plastic bucket capable of holding two gallons (10 litres) with an air space ideally half as much again. You can brew your beers in a much larger bucket with a far greater air space, but take care never to fill it with more than 80% liquid. Once you have standardised your beer-making, you will probably find it more convenient to make at least twice this amount at each attempt, so either buy a bucket designed to hold five gallons (25 litres) or improvise until such time as you have decided on the size of your brews. Do not use a metal bucket, and never allow the beer to come into contact with any metal other than stainless steel, as it will probably be toxic. It is also thought that some of the colourings used in plastics may be poisonous, and for this reason only white plastic is recommended.

Special fermentation buckets with air-tight lids are the best for our purpose. If you do not want to buy one and have a suitable bucket, cover it with a layer of plastic 'cling' film. This material has a wide range of uses both in brewing and wine-making. It acts as a seal, and will not allow air to enter, yet, if the pressure builds up inside the bucket as a result of fermentation, then excess gas is forced through the pores. On other occasions when the pressure above the beer is the same as the atmosphere, gas cannot pass through the barrier.

Never cover buckets with pieces of cloth, or wood or metal trays: all of these will allow germ-carrying air to enter. It is often inconvenient to measure out the liquids, and it is usually impossible to know exactly how much liquid you have prior to fermentation, due to the loss incurred during boiling. These problems can be overcome by measuring volumes of water into the bucket before it is used and marking the position in gallons and half gallons on the side. Another piece of equipment you will probably require is a racking tube, but you can, if you like, omit even this. I know a regular beer-maker of several years standing who always strains the beer after the initial fermentation and who, by steady hand alone, manages to produce beers that regularly win prizes at shows. The general kitchen brewer, however, will find that a racking tube is a good investment. It is best to buy the simplest (and cheapest) of the many types on the market. These are the easiest to operate and, even more important, easy to sterilise. Racking tubes are a constant source of infection unless you are careful. Buy a racking tube consisting of a U-bend about half an inch long (1.25 cm) on one side and a foot to eighteen inches (30–45 cm) on the other with at least six feet (2 metres) of transparent plastic attached to the longer end. Do not use rubber tubing as it is impossible to see if the interior is clean. It also tends to give the beer a rubbery taste.

As well as a racking tube you will need a sieve. You can buy either a special beer sieve or economise by using a piece of cloth, muslin or nylon, inside a colander. Unless you make only kit beers—and even these seem better if the ingredients are boiled—you will need a vessel capable of boiling a quantity of liquid equal to the amount of beer that you wish to make: preserving pans are ideal. A piece of equipment that I have found very useful is a Bruheat bucket, which basically consists of a heating element with variable thermostat inside a heat-resistant plastic bucket in which all the brewing operations requiring elevated temperatures can be performed. Other heating and boiling devices are available, and the home brewer is advised to study them carefully before buying. If you mash your beers you will also require a sugar thermometer.

Some recipes do require specialised equipment. For instance if you are making a lager, you may prefer to conduct a secondary fermentation in demijohns under an airlock. With the large volume involved in beer-making, these are expensive items, and the cost can only really be justified if you are taking a great deal of trouble at all stages. As with so many of the subtle variations in brewing only the enthusiast will be able to taste the improvement. I would suggest that if you have any demijohns and airlocks available which you are not using for winemaking, then try conducting a secondary fermentation in them under airlocks as described in the text and see if you notice any improvement.

How you serve your beer is very much a matter of personal choice, but you will most likely require either a number of bottles and a crown capping machine, or a barrel to put the beer in. Today's beer barrels are virtually fault-free, and there is a very large range to choose from. Dispensing is no problem now that it is possible to buy miniature carbon dioxide bottles at all home brew shops.

Overall, home brewing is simple as long as you understand exactly what you are attempting to do, and this is carefully explained in the following pages.

Throughout the text, units of volume and weight are quoted in Imperial (British) and metric units. To avoid confusion I have equated the pound to a half a kilo and the gallon to 5 litres. In both instances the metric quantity is slightly higher than the imperial equivalent, and the slight extra volume balances the increase in weight. In general, the volume or weight is not critical and slight errors will not detract from the quality of the beer.

The U.S. gallon and pint are slightly smaller than the Imperial equivalents. If you are working with the American system, add an extra pint of water for every gallon given in the ingredients. In general, for mashed beers, one gallon (Imperial) is used for every three pounds of grain at the mashing stage. When using the U.S. units provide 9 pints per three pounds of grain.

Where teaspoons (tsp) are quoted these refer to level spoonfuls.

When using kit beers I have found the methods recommended to be applicable to several different brands. As it has been impossible to test every kit, I would advise you to make the beer according to the manufacturer's instructions for your first brew. Make the next brew according to my variation and decide which you prefer.

Chapter 2

Theory and Commercial Process

Beer

True beers are made from malted barley and hops, and it is in this sense that the word is used throughout the book. The term is also loosely applied to a variety of other drinks made from malt and different herbs. These, by comparison with those made from the hop, are of such poor quality that they will not be mentioned again.

To understand the theory of brewing, it is best to consider the commercial process and adapt it to the kitchen brewery. Today's knowledge has been acquired as a result of trial and error over centuries, and only more recently by scientific investigation by the large commercial breweries. Whilst it is possible to make an acceptable drink by carefully following a set of relatively simple instructions—and the kit manufacturers have gone to considerable trouble to ensure that modern home brewing is an easy operation—if you wish to make beers individually tailored to your own palate you may find it necessary to change the recipes slightly.

The search for perfection can only be conducted by the brewer himself. He may have to make certain adjustments in his method because the local water supply is not ideal, or because he has a limited time to spare or because he cannot obtain a certain ingredient, although this is seldom a problem today. This does not mean that the majority of brewers will have to produce their own methods and recipes: amongst those provided there should be some to cater for all tastes, but it is always better, should the need arise, to be able to make your own decisions. This is only possible if you understand the fundamentals of brewing, but a detailed knowledge of chemistry is not necessary. No scientific knowledge is required other than that found in the text.

There are home brewers of many years standing who feel that a study of brewing practice is a waste of time, and wish only to make their favourite brew in the shortest possible time with the minimum of effort. Perhaps you have tasted their beers and found them good, but remember 'experts' never give you their failures to try or find it necessary to mention them. These people are at a loss when something does go wrong, which is often the case when you embark on a venture with insufficient knowledge. Moreover, they are in no position to take advantage of any new equipment or ingredients that may come on to the market designed to make our task easier. Home brewing is now such a popular pastime that new products are becoming available virtually all the time; some are excellent whilst others are just a waste of money. A lack of basic knowledge puts you at the mercy of the salesmen, whose goods may have nothing to commend them other than the wording on the packet.

Again, when you give beer to your friends, they may not only ask you how the beer was made, but also about the brewing process itself, and it is important to be able to answer them.

It is worth remembering that the person who knows most about brewing often makes the best beer.

Making Malt

Food is stored in barley as starch, a non-fermentable carbohydrate which is useless in the production of alcohol. Barley cannot use the starch directly as food, it has to be converted first into a sugar, which is done by means of special enymes—chemical agents that change the structure of materials. The brewer makes use of these by allowing the seeds to germinate, producing the enzymes in the process and also facilitating the removal of the starch which, if not converted to sugar, produces an irremovable haze. The grains are then heated to a sufficiently high temperature to kill the growing shoot, but not high enough to destroy the delicate enzymes. The resulting product is termed malt and is the most important ingredient in brewing.

Malt is made by first steeping the barley in water, draining off the excess and spreading the soaked grain on the malting-house floor. The humidity and temperature are both carefully controlled, and when the first growth emerges the mass is turned to allow oxygen and nitrogen free passage and to ensure that the roots do not mat. It is essential that the seeds are allowed to germinate sufficiently to allow maximum enzyme production, but not for too long, or the plant will begin to use up the sugar that it has already produced. The brewer needs this sugar for the production of alcohol.

Germination is stopped by light roasting and again the conditions are critical. If the grain is left in the oven too long, or is allowed to reach too high a temperature, then the delicate enzymes will be destroyed. Pale malts retain virtually all of their enzyme activity. In dark malts it is often completely destroyed, although sometimes they are heated to a temperature at which they will retain some of their activity. However, home brewers should assume that dark malts will not be able to convert their starch into sugar, and should always use at least 75%–80% pale malt to provide sufficient enzymes to change the starch into sugar.

The traditional method of malting described above is still practised by many breweries, but with the tendency towards bulk production, many are changing over to an automatic process in which the steeped grains are placed in a rotating drum which turns the sprouting grains mechanically, and can subsequently be emptied automatically into the oven.

It is virtually impossible for the kitchen brewer to produce his own malt satisfactorily, for not only must the conditions—the humidity, the free passage of air, the period of time and the roasting temperature—be correct, but the quality of the barley is also critical.

Barley, and less frequently, wheat, are the only grains which are malted because they alone produce sufficient enzymes for the conversion of starches to sugars. Rye and oats are roasted for stouts, but (like the gelatinised adjuncts of flake maize and rice) they contribute virtually nothing to the enzyme activity. Not all barley is suitable for malting as it must have a low nitrogen content. Nitrogen is a constituent of the fibrous protein material of the grain, and this has to be low for two reasons. A large amount of protein in the grain means that the carbohydrate level will be low and make the process less efficient. But, more importantly, the nitrogen will form a haze in the beer, which, like the starch haze, is impossible to clear. The nitrogen content is to some extent responsible for heading characteristics and for this reason alone it needs careful monitoring. In the United Kingdom only barley with a nitrogen content of less than 1.7% is used for malting whilst in the United States up to 2.2% is tolerated.

Brewing has developed independently in many different parts of the world. As well as the obvious recipe differences between the beers of different countries, subtle differences such as the nitrogen content of the barley, malting and mashing temperatures, hop treatment and hop varieties, contribute a great deal to the final character. For these reasons you may never be able to copy a particular style of beer exactly, however careful you are in compounding the recipe. In most instances the approximation will be sufficiently close that after a few weeks you will think that your beer is the real one.

Top quality brewer's malt is now generally available, and can be used to produce excellent beers, but this method is more time-consuming and requires more work and equipment than using wort concentrates.

Mashing

In the commercial brewery malt is transferred to a large copper (or stainless steel) vessel, the mash tun, and heated with water. (The brewer only uses the term water for the washing liquid, always describing that used to make his precious beer as liquor.)

The malt is heated with the liquor at between 147–152°F (64–67.5°C). This temperature is critical because of the reactions that the starch undergoes.

Starch is dissolved out of the grains—although some reaction does occur in the grains themselves—and is converted to the virtually non-fermentable carbohydrate dextrin by one of the enzymes present. A second enzyme converts the dextrins to the fermentable sugar maltose. The temperatures at which these two enzymes are most active are 150°F (65°C) for the starch-to-dextrin conversion and 135°F (57°C) for the dextrin-to-maltose reaction. 150°F is the upper limit for the latter conversion and some dextrins will always be present in the liquid—the higher the mashing temperature the higher the percentage of dextrins. Since it is not destroyed by fermentation, the dextrin will remain present in the final brew as dissolved solids and give the beer body. It is the ratio of dextrin to maltose that fixes the mashing temperature. A change of only two or three degrees will have a noticeable effect, and this is the reason why different types of beer are mashed at different temperatures. Temperature control often worries the home brewer, but since a standardised product is not absolutely essential and providing reasonable care is taken it does not present that great a problem. (Indeed slight variations, providing they are not drastic, add to the interest of beer making).

After the grain has been maintained at this temperature for 1½–2 hours, it is tested to ensure that there is no free starch present, and the liquid now termed wort (pronounced *wurt*) is filtered off into the boiler.

Sparging

The grains at the bottom of the mash tun will

Summary of the Biochemistry of Brewing

1. Malting House Floor
   Release of enzymes and the conversion of some of the starch to sugar

2. Kiln
   Roasting stops growth and develops the flavour of the malt

3. Mash Tun
   Conversion of starch to dextrins by higher temperature acting enzymes
   Conversion of dextrins to maltose by lower temperature acting enzymes
   Dissolving of sugars and nitrogenous materials for head retention out of the grains

4. Boiler
   Destroys enzymes responsible for converting starch to sugar
   Dissolves the acids responsible for bitterness, and the aromatic substances out of the hops
   Clearing process commences (hot break)

5. Shock Cooling
   Completes the clearing process (cold break)

6. Fermentation
   Converts the sugars (maltose and sucrose) to alcohol and carbon dioxide

7. Conditioning and Maturation
   Conditioning carbon dioxide generated
   Yeast sediment clears
   Chemical interaction completes flavour formation
   Heading characteristics develop

form the filter bed through which the wort, a thick sticky liquid with a high concentration of dissolved sugars, passes.

The viscosity of the liquid causes much of it to adhere to the surface of the grains. It would be wasteful to discard this sugar-rich liquid, so the grains are *sparged*, by spraying them with fine jets of water, until the filtered liquor, which is heated to the mashing temperature, no longer contains significant amounts of dissolved sugar. Care is taken both that the distribution of liquor is correct, so that all grains are washed equally, and that over-sparging, in which the unconverted starch remaining in the grains will be leached out, does not occur.

It should be apparent that there are many pitfalls in the mashing and sparging processes. Fortunately, by buying worts, concentrated down to a treacle-like consistency, we can let the professionals do the job for us. These concentrates are made by boiling off the water from the wort at greatly reduced pressure and temperature. At the lower temperature the enzymes are not destroyed and retain all their activity. Such extracts are called *diastatic* and may be used either to reconstitute a straight wort by the addition of water, or added with grains to a mash tun—a process that is used today by commercial breweries—when the enzyme activity is essential to complete the mashing.

By evaporating all the water from the wort, powdered malt is produced. This is obviously a more expensive product, but is a useful additive to many beers, and excellent ales can be brewed from it.

Hops

The hop plant, a member of the same family as both cannabis and hemp, carries its flowers on the current year's growth, the bines being cut down yearly. Male and female flowers, (only the latter are used in brewing) are borne on separate plants. The female hop cone consists of an outer smaller layer of plates, termed bracts, which are worthless, and an inner layer called bracteoles. At the base of the bracteoles are the lupulin glands, which contain the resins and essential oils needed in beer. As these glands are only fully developed when the cone is ripe, and rapidly deteriorate thereafter, the time of harvesting is critical. If there are male plants growing in the vicinity, seeds develop at the base of the bracteole as a result of wind pollination. Fertilised hops are much lower in essential oils and resins than unfertilised flowers, and consequently far less economical to use. In many countries seedless hops are grown by destroying all male plants but where wild hops exist, as in the British Isles, this is impossible, and wind pollination occurs.

As soon as the hops are gathered, they are transferred to an oast house, where they are dried at 150°F (62°C) for ten hours. This drying process stops moulds attacking the damp tissue. In some countries, including Britain, sulphur is burnt in the kiln during the drying, this gives the hops a bright yellowish tinge which helps with their evaluation. It does not appear to affect the quality.

Boiling

The combined liquids from the mashing and sparging processes are then boiled with hops. During the boiling process the enzymes are destroyed and the ratio of dextrins to sugar is irreversibly fixed. At the same time essential oils and acids, which give the beer much of its characteristic flavour, are extracted from the

hops. It is thought that hop oils help to preserve beer, although there is some doubt about this. The importance of using sound hops in the correct proportion cannot be over emphasised, but since it is just as easy to buy good hops as bad, make sure that you buy only the most suitable.

The hopped wort is usually boiled for 1½ hours. This not only extracts the maximum amount of oils from the hops, but brings about complex reactions in the liquid. During the boiling, solid material coagulates and is deposited, resulting in a clarification of the liquid. This is called the 'hot break'. The effectiveness of natural clearing processes depends very much on the type of beer being made, and Irish moss, a substance derived from dried sea algae, is sometimes added to the wort. The ingredient in Irish moss that is responsible for the clarification is *carrageenan* and this substance is sometimes sold as 'carrageenan moss'. It is also called copper finings, because it is added in the boiler or copper.

In addition to the hops any sugar is added at the beginning of the boil. In some breweries not all the hops are added at the start, with up to a quarter being added about half an hour before boiling is completed. This increases the aroma of the drink, many of the fragrant compounds being lost as a result of prolonged boiling.

When the wort is added a second deposit of gum-like material forms. This is called the 'cold break'. At this stage the wort should be reasonably clear and all deposits are removed by filtration.

Hopped worts are condensed in the same manner as unhopped worts and these are the basis of the kit beers that are sold.

The process that I have explained is a simplification of the preparation of worts, but it allows us to identify four possible starting materials for the kitchen brewer.

1. Malt
2. Diastatic Malt Extract
3. Dried Malt
4. Hopped Malt extracts

Chapter 3
Fermentation

In the previous chapter we considered the commercial brewing process and how its products can be adapted to our purpose: once the hopped wort has been prepared, whether in the brewery or at home, it must be fermented. At this stage there are no real differences between the two techniques, except that of scale.

It is often mistakenly thought that fermenting a beer wort is the same process as treating a wine must. However, despite the many similarities, there are clear distinctions between the two processes and they should be considered separately. When fermenting a wine it is usually necessary to obtain a high alcohol concentration of between 12% and 16%. The high alcohol content of wine is not only an integral part of the drink, but is also essential to preserve the drink, which may take several years to reach its full potential. Beers do not require long maturation periods and unlike wines are meant to be drunk in reasonably large quantities which of course is not possible if they are too strong. Usually the first aim of home brewers is to make their beers extra strong. This is very easy—all you need to do is to add extra sugar—but the resulting drinks are not very palatable and result in terrible hangovers. The alcohol content is a very important aspect of brewing, but it is only one aspect, and the strength should never be confused with the quality of the drink. Surely it is better to be able to drink a second (or third) pint and not have to limit your intake because the alcoholic content of the beer is too high? Nevertheless, home brewed beers do tend to be stronger than their commercial counterparts and you will usually drink far less. If you want a beer to quench your thirst on a hot day in the garden without falling asleep afterwards, then make some of the low alcohol beers such as the bitters that have only a relatively low malt and sugar content. Even lower alcohol beers can be obtained by omitting the sugar entirely, but such drinks seldom keep for long, and are far more likely to become infected.

Yeast

The sugar extracted from the wort is converted into alcohol by using yeast, and while it is doing this several other chemical reactions occur. These lesser processes, which depend to a very large extent on the type of yeast used and the temperature at which fermentation is conducted, have a very great effect on the final taste and flavour of the beer. It is important that the correct type of yeast is used and that the fermentation is correctly conducted if you want to brew the best beers.

Wine Yeast

Again, the differences between wine- and beer-making are important. While both need to use yeasts which do not produce off flavours, only wine yeast needs to possess a high tolerance to alcohol. Yeasts for brewing must form a hard crust at the bottom of a bottle so that the sediment is not transferred to the glass when poured. Long before wines are drunk the yeast is removed from the liquid, usually as a light mobile sediment. This removal is not practical with beers (unless you use 'Beerbrite' caps) which must finish their fermentation in the bottle to avoid flatness. Consequently, wine yeasts are not generally suitable for beer-making, and although one manufacturer told me that his beers could be successfully fermented with wine yeasts, this is not a generally held view.

Wine yeasts are required for making barley wines however, and their alcohol content can be as high as 12%: these beers should always be carefully poured.

Baker's Yeasts

Since baker's yeasts were originally obtained from brewery skimmings it is often thought that today's special bread yeasts would be ideal for brewing. Unfortunately most baker's yeasts are cultured in a medium of molasses and the yeast cells, which quickly mutate and adapt to any change in the environment, have increased the size of their cell walls so that they can process the abundance of nutrients quickly. These changes have resulted in the loss of the important characteristics of flavour and crust formation. It is not advisable therefore to make beer from baker's yeast. It is thought that baker's yeast, and other yeasts derived from them, are responsible for the objectionable yeasty taste of many home brewed beers.

However the reverse does not follow: bread can be made using the yeast skimmings of beer, as we found out one year during a baker's strike when we could obtain no alternative.

General Purpose Yeasts

All-purpose yeasts can be used for bread, wine- and beer-making, but it is far better to use a strain bred specifically for the purpose.

Beer Yeasts

Specially cultured beer yeasts for use by home brewers are now easily obtainable. Without a doubt these give the best results.

There are two types of beer yeast and it is advisable always to use the correct one if possible. However should it not be obtainable, or should you wish to buy only one yeast for your brewing, then it is possible to use the 'wrong' yeast and still get the right result.

Top-Fermenting Yeasts These form a very thick layer at the top of the yeast, due to the yeast cells floating to the surface. These yeasts have always been used to brew British beers, and are recommended for all beers except lagers.

Bottom Fermenting Yeasts Brewers have for generations sought the secrets of their more successful rivals and attributed their success to the water, yeast or other factors (but never to their own lack of skill). Some of the finest lagers were made at Carlsberg. A sample of the yeast, which was different from that used by other beer-makers, was taken away and is used today throughout the world to make this very distinctive type of beer. As the name implies, the yeast ferments at the bottom of the vessel and does not throw such a large head as the top-acting yeasts.

There are other differences between the two yeasts, lager yeasts require slightly higher acid levels and generally work better at temperatures 10°F (5°C) lower than those favoured by top-acting yeasts. As a result of this lower temperature fermentation takes longer to reach completion.

When making country wines there is little point in using the same yeast as the vintners do, because there is a major difference in the ingredients. But with brewing we are using starting materials very like our commercial counterparts', so there is possibly a great deal to be gained by employing strains that have been carefully bred over several years. If you wish, (and it is by no means essential) you can easily obtain two of the best known beer yeasts.

For little more than the cost of a packet of yeast you can buy either a bottle of Guinness, whose yeast is ideal for making Irish stouts, or Worthington White Label, which is suitable for all pale and light ales and can also be used to produce very good browns and milds. These two beers are living, that is to say the carbon dioxide is generated through secondary fermentation by yeast in the bottle, unlike most beers where the yeast is filtered off to afford a clear, easily-handled drink. Living beers always demand more respect than artificially carbonated ones.

To produce sufficient yeast for fermentation from a pint or half a pint of beer, it is necessary to make up a starter bottle two days before the yeast is required. Pour the Guinness into the glass, except for the bottom layer of yeast which should be transferred to a sterilised milk bottle (or kept in the beer bottle). Add 2 oz (50 gm) of dried pale malt (or sugar) and the tip of a teaspoon of citric acid and make up the total volume to a quarter of a pint with tap water.

Cover the top of the container with a piece of plastic kitchen film. Do not use cotton wool as a covering, because this gives no protection at all. Place the starter bottle in a temperature of 65–70°F (18.5–21°C).

Drink the Guinness or Worthington.

After 24–48 hours a voluminous head will develop. At this stage the whole of the liquid including any sediment should be added to the beer.

Theoretically any real ale–that is beer whose heading gas is obtained by fermentation in the barrel–can be treated in the same way. All that is required is to buy a pint of draught beer as an off-sale from a public house, take it home and allow the yeast to settle out. Not only is there often only a small crop of yeast–the beer would have been cloudy otherwise–but in order to obtain it, the beer must be left in a cold place overnight. The beer, by now undrinkable, is poured off the following morning.

A starter bottle is made up from the sediment. Unfortunately this often results in infections developing, which spoil the beer.

Most brewers will find it more convenient to use one of the dried beer yeasts or better still a liquid culture which avoids the trouble of making a starter bottle. I never use starter bottles these days. The theory is that by activating the yeast in a starter bottle, it forms a carbon dioxide layer more rapidly. This stops the bacteria which thrive in air from attacking and spoiling the beer. Whilst maintaining sterile conditions is essential, this particular form of protection is unnecessary.

Many kit beer manufacturers provide a sachet of dried yeast which they instruct the brewer to add straight to the wort at the recommended temperature. If there was any real danger of infection they could not afford to omit this from their instructions!

Kit Yeast

Where hopped wort extracts are provided with yeasts, it is safe to assume that they are suitable for that particular kit.

The Action of the Yeast

Yeast reproduces by the division of cells; several cells join together to form a cluster. These clusters are dried, the outer ones lose all their moisture and form a hard crust. Under these conditions the yeast can be kept for months, the actual time depending upon the storage conditions. The sealed packets in which it is sold affords ample protection, and you are unlikely to get dead yeast from a good supplier who has a rapid turnover.

Check the yeast clusters by rubbing one between your forefinger and thumb, being careful not to handle the other grains and risk contamination. If the cluster does not break easily then it is still alive, but if it crumbles to dust then it is probably too old and should not be used. As soon as the yeast comes into contact with a suitable growing medium, then moisture passes through the outer hard skin of dead cells and the live yeast regains its activity.

Yeast obtains its energy from sugar and in the process produces two byproducts, alcohol and carbon dioxide. Before the yeast can change sugar into alcohol it must convert it into a form from which it can feed–a process termed inversion. The most important brewing sugar is maltose which is obtained from malt, the yeast inverts this to glucose at its cell wall. Similarly sucrose, (better known as household sugar) cannot be assimilated by yeast, so it converts this to a mixture of fructose and glucose which it can use. Once the sugar has been inverted to the correct form the yeast converts it by enzyme action to alcohol.

Initial Fermentation

Two distinct stages occur in the fermentation process, the first, initial fermentation, is when the yeast is breeding rapidly and is at its most active. This vigorous activity will be seen as a voluminous white head consisting mainly of yeast cells at the top of the liquid. For this process oxygen is required, hence the alternative name– aerobic fermentation. Ideally during this period the fermentation vessel should never be more than two-thirds full. A larger air space will not be harmful.

The time taken for this head to form will depend upon many factors, such as the amount of yeast originally added, the temperature, and whether a top- or bottom-fermenting yeast was employed. Bottom-fermenting yeasts produce far less head than top-fermenting types, and as they prefer lower temperatures take longer to produce the beer.

Carbon dioxide, which is much heavier than air, and which stays just above the liquid, is responsible for the bubbles in the head. This blanket of gas, which effectively removes the air from the surface of the liquid, protects the wort from attack by spoilage yeasts. These spoilage yeasts require far larger quantities of air than is now available to take advantage of the conditions created for the beer yeast.

Yeast multiplies very rapidly during the early stages, but after a fixed period of time the number of yeast cells present will be related to the amount of yeast originally added. Consequently the speed at which the sugar is used up, the overall fermentation time, will also be related to the amount of yeast provided. As fermentation proceeds the number of yeast cells will reach a maximum based on the amount of water, sugar, other nutrients, and air in the container. In theory, however small the quantity of yeast added, the colony will increase in size to ferment out the wort. But it is essential to provide a reasonable amount of yeast so that it builds up to a maximum as quickly as possible, in order to provide the protective blanket of carbon dioxide.

Yeast is usually sold in satchets sufficient to make either two gallons or five. No harm will be done by adding all of the yeast from a packet designed for making five gallons to two gallons: it may even slightly speed up the fermentation. But by using a two gallon size for a five gallon brew you are in danger of providing insufficient yeast and leaving the beer open to infection.

If you are using yeast from a drum add a teaspoonful to a two gallon batch and twice as much to a five gallon ferment. However it is only advisable to use yeast from drums if you are having regular brews.

Use a fresh sachet of yeast for each fermentation, because once the air-tight seal has been broken it is open to entry by other yeasts which will breed as rapidly as the desired strain. Also moisture is bound to enter the yeast, accelerating its decomposition and reducing its storage time.

The duration of the voluminous head during the initial fermentation will depend on the same factors that influenced its formation. During the period of its existence it protects the liquid so fully that the commercial breweries, who cannot afford to have one failure, leave the fermenting vat uncovered. It is usually more convenient at home, especially if you do not want the house to smell like a brewery, to cover this liquid by using a fermentation bucket with an air-tight lid. This also minimises any danger from infection should you fail to notice that the vigorous fermentation has come to an end.

During this initial fermentation brown gum-like deposits are formed due to side reactions. These deposits and the yeast head will, if left in contact with the liquid, impart a bitter taste to the drink. It is essential to skim the excess yeast from the surface of the liquid and remove the gum which tends to adhere to the side of the vessel. Scraping the side with a spoon ensures that all of the gum is removed. This removal should be performed on the third and sixth day. However, individual brews differ considerably, so whenever there is an excess growth, or the appearance of gum, remove it.

Do not take this to extremes by removing the yeast daily, because these are the cells that are responsible for the fermentation. You will only slow up the process and increase the risk of infection. For this reason, always leave some of the white head after skimming, checking that there is no gum in it.

During the initial fermentation stage the yeast requires air, and it is important to stir the liquid each time the yeast is removed, to dissolve as much of the gas as possible. This process is termed 'rousing' the beer. The initial fermentation stage has finished when you can no longer see a fresh head developing, only a slower steady evolution of bubbles rather like the head in a glass of beer that has been poured for some time.

Secondary Fermentation

The next stage, secondary fermentation, occurs when the yeast colony has built up to a maximum and no longer takes its oxygen from the air, but from that chemically combined in the sugar. This is called *anaerobic* (without air) fermentation. With low alcohol drinks, such as beer, the majority of the sugar will have been converted to alcohol at this stage, but it is important to ensure that there is no fermentable sugar still present, other than the carefully controlled amount added before bottling. When beer is bottled the necessary carbon dioxide will be provided by priming it with sugar. This quantity must be exact, as if there is not enough the beer will be flat and without a head. Should there be too much sugar in the liquid then this will result in a very high gas pressure in the bottles with the risk that the liquid will spurt out of the bottle on opening like a fountain, covering wallpaper, carpet, furniture and even ceilings, or possibly even the bottle will explode.

During the secondary fermentation stage, carbon dioxide is produced at a sufficient rate to protect the yeast from bacterial attack. Since these germs thrive in the presence of air, it is necessary to ensure that they do not have a chance to establish themselves in the brew. One method is to remove virtually all air by transferring the liquid to a demijohn, ensuring that the liquid level is within two inches (5 cm) of the top of the container. If you find the level is lower than this, top up with water—unless large gaps occur in which case you must fill up with a solution made by dissolving 4 oz (100 gm) sugar or preferably dried malt extract in a pint (½ litre) of water. Fit an airlock, filled with water, to the demijohn.

The progress of fermentation can be considered complete when no further bubbles of gas can be seen escaping from the airlock. After two days check the gravity of the beer with an hydrometer. It should read between 1.010 and 1.000 depending upon the quantity of dextrin present. If the value is higher than this, then the fermentation will have stopped and it will be necessary to restart it.

Check that the temperature is 65°–70°F (18.5–21°C), as low temperature is the most common cause of problems. If it is too low, place in the correct environment when the beer will usually start working again. If fermentation does not restart, transfer the beer to a second demijohn by pouring slowly. This allows the maximum amount of carbon dioxide dissolved in the beer to escape and be replaced by air, which will help reactivate the yeast.

Should this treatment fail, and it seldom does, pour half of the liquid into a second demijohn, add a fresh supply of yeast to each container and fit them with airlocks. Within two days the beer should have started working again. Allow the beer to continue to ferment in the half-filled containers. Do not recombine, as such arrested fermentation is probably the sign of a beer which is deficient in nutrients and which may stop again. Unlike wine with its delicate flavours, beer is not readily spoiled by oxidation. The danger comes from infection.

It is quite common to avoid the use of demijohns by allowing the secondary fermentation to continue in the same vessel that was used for the initial stage without disturbance. This method is totally satisfactory, except for barley wines, provided that you complete the secondary fermentation within ten to fourteen days, and that the container is covered. After about a fortnight the dead yeast cells will have begun decomposing and will begin to give the beer an off flavour. Therefore the beer should be racked off immediately. As well as saving time, this method saves expenditure on the relatively expensive demijohns. Using this approach it is necessary to take samples periodically and test with a hydrometer. When the gravity does not drop for three consecutive days all the fermentable sugar may be considered to have been converted to alcohol.

The amount of air entering the beer when samples are taken is usually insufficient to allow germs to become established, although it increases with the number of samples taken. With this method 'stuck' ferments are almost unknown, and problems are seldom encountered providing the time-scale is observed.

On balance, fermentation conducted with a large space above the liquid is probably better with all beers except lager and barley wine. Many factors differ in the lagering process, the most important of which is the slow, relatively low temperature fermentation.

With low temperature fermentation a far longer secondary fermentation stage is necessary, (often a month to six weeks). Conducting such a fermentation in the same vessel, with the yeast still present from the initial fermentation, can lead to evil beers. If you wish to make lagers in a large vessel, fermentation should be conducted at the same temperature as employed for other beers. When lagers are made in this way there is only a slight loss in quality.

Barley wines require an even longer fermentation period, often of about three months, and must be conducted in a demijohn under an airlock.

Once the secondary fermentation is complete, it is necessary to restart the process in the bottle to condition the beer. This aspect of secondary fermentation is identical in all respects to the preceding stage and occurs only at the correct temperature.

Temperature

The temperature at which fermentation is conducted is as important, perhaps more so, than the type of yeast used. Quite often this is a factor ignored by home brewers, who find that they can make beer in the summer simply by relying on the ambient temperature and in the winter by depending upon the central heating. Fortunately the temperature which we like to live in is suitable, if not ideal, for yeasts; however, if there are large fluctuations this can result in lower quality beers, and even stuck fermentation. Depending upon the type, yeasts will ferment sugar from just above freezing point to about 90–100°F (32–37°C). The higher the temperature the quicker the fermentation ceases, but the minor reactions accompanying the process, so important in terms of the final flavours, are dependent on temperature as well as yeast type, and it is these processes rather than the conversion of sugar to alcohol that dictate the temperature that must be employed. In addition, if the fermentation is conducted at too high a temperature, then many of the very delicate flavourings of the hops will be volatilised off, and this loss will completely alter the characteristics of the drink. Should the temperature be too low, then fermentation will take too long, tying up valuable equipment and possibly resulting in stuck ferments. Although yeast is relatively tolerant to adverse conditions— the ideal conditions should be provided at this stage, in order to build up the important protective head as quickly as possible. As the alcohol, (which poisons the yeast, ultimately killing it when the concentration reaches a volume between 12 and 16% dependent upon yeast type) builds up, the plant finds it difficult to survive. Unless the temperature is kept up to a minimum value, 60–65°F (15–18.5°C) for top-acting yeast, 55–60°F (13–15°C) for bottom-acting yeast) fermentation can cease prematurely in small containers that do not provide their own internal thermal insulation. The temperature should be maintained at the same level during primary and secondary fermentation and for the first week of the conditioning period.

In most houses it is possible to keep the fermenting liquid within the recommended range without too much difficulty. If however, this does present a problem, then *depending upon the amount of beer you want* you can either make a fermenting cabinet or use one of the various heaters on the market.

The home brewer will find that in general he will not need to make more than one batch of beer at a time, as opposed to the wine-maker who has to contend with three months fermentation period, and so will be able to use the various heaters and mantles that are perfectly adequate for individual brews.

By using top-acting yeast it is possible to ferment both beers and wine together as they require a similar temperature—to do this successfully it is preferable to have a fermentation cabinet. Before attempting to make such a cabinet you must decide on the quantities of beer you require. Until you have discovered which recipes and variations suit your particular palate it is advisable to make only 2 gallon (10 litres) batches—smaller amounts are impractical—but later you will find that it is more efficient to brew in 5 gallon (25 litres) batches. The same caution should be applied before buying any equipment, do not spend large amounts of money until you are relatively sure about the scale on which you intend to operate.

To construct a fermentation cabinet first decide on the size of the container or containers and whether you intend to use it in conjuction with wine. Make a box slightly larger than the containers so that they can be easily moved in or out, with either front- or top-opening doors. Bore a small hole through one side and thread a piece of electrical flex through it. Then connect a thermostat (the kind used in an aquarium), followed by a small heater used with the same apparatus. A 25W or 50W bulb can be used in place of a heater although these do tend to burn out rather quickly. Both fermentation cabinets and the specially designed heating mantles sold for the same purpose are very cheap to run, but the cost can be lowered still further by lining the cabinet with fireproof polystyrene tiles. A layer of baking foil stuck to the tiles will minimise losses through radiation. The construction of an insulated box, made along similar lines, will give the same effect if you are using a mantle.

I was talking recently to a beermaker from Queensland, Australia, where they usually have to lower the temperature rather than raise it. For making lager, the country's most popular beer, keen brewers buy a second-hand refrigerator and run it at a temperature just above freezing point. After the initial fermentation has started, the beer is placed in the refrigerator. It may not be practical to adopt this approach in all tropical regions, and it is probably not necessary or desirable to take the temperature so low because it can result in stuck ferments. But it is important to conduct the fermentation in the coldest part of the house.

The temperature at which fermentation should be conducted must be between the lower limit that allows fermentation to continue and the upper limit above which the quality of the beer is lost.

During the fermentation process, a considerable quantity of heat is generated, and the temperature of the liquid rises. Here we notice a major difference in the commercial and kitchen techniques. Brewery vats are very large, and with

Table I

Recommended Fermentation Temperatures for Home Brewing

Yeast Type	Use with	Temperature if not using heater		Setting for thermostat of heater
		Maximum	Minimum	
Top Acting Yeast	Pale Ales, Bitters	75 F†	60 F	65 F
	Brown Stouts	21 C	15 C	17 C
Bottom Acting Yeast	Lagers	63 F†	50 F*	55 F
		14 C	10 C	13 C
Wine Yeast	Barley Wine	70 F†	65 F	65 F
		21 C	17 C	17 C

† This value may be exceeded by not more than 5°F (2.5°C) for very short periods.
* Yeast will usually tolerate a drop of 10°F (5.0°C) below this value, providing the correct value is restored within a few hours.

---

such a high ratio of liquid to surface area heat losses tend to be slow. Temperature rises quickly in the vat, and it is usual to cool the brew by means of water pipes when it reaches the low seventies (about 22°C). In the smaller vessels used in the kitchen not only is this unnecessary, but it would slow down the fermentation.

Acidity

Yeast requires a slightly acidic environment. If this acidity is missing not only might the yeast die but, if it lives, fermentation will be slower and the beer will have an acceptably bitter taste. Most waters are sufficiently acidic for the yeast to start working, and once the process has commenced the carbon dioxide, which itself is acid, will ensure that conditions remain suitable. Far lower levels of acidity are required in brewing than in wine-making where the acid contributes to the astringency of the drink. In most areas the question of acidity can be ignored, and you should adjust the acid level only if you experience difficulties in starting the yeast working.

If you do have trouble with the initial fermentation contact the local water authority and ask them for the pH of the water. pH is a scientific scale for measuring acidity, in which the lower the pH the higher the acidity. If the pH of the water is below 6.0, then this is not the cause of your problems. If the pH is above this figure, especially if it exceeds 7.0 when there is no residual acid present, it is necessary to add acid. Lager yeasts seem to benefit from a slightly higher acid level. One level teaspoonful per two gallons (10 litres) will do no harm to most waters used for brewing, otherwise add acid according to the correction chart. The most suitable acid is lactic but should you be unable to obtain it, citric acid may be used instead. The advantage of lactic acid is that if you exceed the recommended amount, its taste is so mild that it does not impart a noticeable acid taste to the beer, whereas excess citric acid produces the characteristic flavour of lemons in the drink.

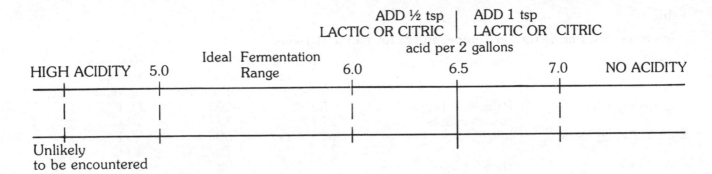

ADD ½ tsp | ADD 1 tsp
LACTIC OR CITRIC | LACTIC OR CITRIC
acid per 2 gallons

Ideal Fermentation
Range

HIGH ACIDITY   5.0   6.0   6.5   7.0   NO ACIDITY

Unlikely
to be encountered

Due to the complex nature of the various tap waters it is not possible to predict what the new acid levels will be. This is not important, all that matters is that there will be sufficient acid to start fermentation after treatment.

Home brewers tend to worry too much about the composition of water and its acid level, and are too ready to add extra acid, when in most instances it is neither necessary or desirable.

Too high an acid can result in lower amounts of carbon dioxide being dissolved in the beer—there is a total acid solubility and it is far better to have a high carbon dioxide level and a low added acid level than the reverse. It is not advisable to go to the extent of testing the acidity for yourself, with pH papers or acid kits—the results from either can be virtually meaningless without the background of scientific knowledge to interpret them.

Nutrients

Yeast needs certain additional nutrients besides sugar if it is to function efficiently. However nitrogen, which is the most important, and other compounds, such as phosphates, are already present in the barley in sufficient quantities to

make further additions unnecessary. The only exception to this is if a barley wine fermentation sticks. Add half a teaspoonful of ammonium phosphate or yeast nutrient per gallon before attempting to restart the ferment.

Do not worry about getting all the conditions just right for fermentation. All you need to do is to select a suitable yeast and provide a reasonable temperature. Tap water is usually ideal for brewing.

During fermentation, the beer should be skimmed and roused and all the precautions taken to ensure that it does not become infected. If you follow these simple rules then you are unlikely to experience any problems.

Chapter 4
Ingredients

Walk into any home brew shop and you will find the shelves full of beer-making ingredients. Home brewing has become such a popular pastime that an industry has developed around it, preparing and marketing every conceivable ingredient. If you do not live near a home brew shop, you can always purchase in bulk when you do find a shop, or by post from a specialist mail order firm. Fortunately, you will only need a few ingredients which will vary according to the beers and their flavours. You should pay careful attention to the type and quality of the ingredients that you use. Drinkable beers can be made from virtually any malt and hops, but the best beers are only produced if the right ingredients are used in the correct amounts.

Malt

With the exception of lager malts, all malts are prepared from green, undried malt. Malts differ because of the temperature and time of roasting. These differences not only affect the beer's flavour but also the method of brewing and type of beer. The flavour develops and the colour darkens as the kilning temperature increases.

Pale Malt

This is the most important ingredient in brewing and should represent at least 75—80% of all solid materials used to make a wort with the exception of sugar.

Pale malt is made by kilning green malt to 170–180°F (80°C). At this temperature, none of the enzymes necessary to convert starch to sugar are destroyed.

Pale malts tend to produce lightly flavoured beers. Most beers are a mixture of malts and the percentage of pale malt is at its highest in light ales and lowest in brown ales and stouts. However pale malt is predominant even in these drinks.

Dark Malts

This name is applied to the grains produced by kilning to a temperature of 200–230°F (100°C). Dark malts give the colour and flavour to brown and mild beers. At the lower end of the temperature range a great deal of enzyme activity is retained, but with a consequent loss of flavour. In large-scale production these malts are sometimes kilned for a specific recipe, another reason why without the actual malts we cannot hope to exactly reproduce a commercial brew. It is possible to overcome this to some extent by slightly adjusting the ratio of pale and dark malts. Even if you are satisfied with the quality of the beer, try a 5% adjustment to see the effect. Only by doing this can you keep improving.

Black Malt

Black malt is largely responsible for the characteristic flavour of certain dark beers. It has no enzyme activity, and its only other use is in very strong old ales and stouts. It is made by kilning green malt to about 400°F (200°C).

Since the three malts differ only in the kilning temperature, in theory it should be possible to buy pale malt and make the other types by heating in the oven. This, however, is not easy because for the best results malt must contain a low, but significant, amount of moisture. Different oven sizes, the thickness of malt layers and other factors make it impossible to suggest drying times. When malt is stored correctly it should not absorb any moisture from the atmosphere. If it does it is described as 'slack', and is unsuitable for mashing. If your malt has gone slack, try drying it out in the oven for one hour at 180°F (80°C) for pale malts, 210°F (100°C) for dark malts and 400°F (200°C) for black malts.

Crystal Malts

In the production of the pale, dark and black malts, green malt is roasted in three stages and great care is taken to ensure each time that the moisture content drops to a specified level before the temperature is raised. Failure to do this results in the grain becoming stewed; the water dissolves out the starches and sugars, and the enzyme is killed by what is, in effect, super-heated steam.

Limited stewing is employed in the production of crystal malts. On cooling, the sugars crystallise to give a glassy mass. Crystal malt can be used as an additive to provide sugars together with flavour and colour. When used in small amounts to replace household sugar, it greatly improves the quality of the beer. As it is high in sugars as a result of a mashing process within the grain, the brewer needs only dissolve the sugar out of the crushed grains with hot water. Unlike pure malts, crystal malt is useful whether the beer is made from grain or extracts and is probably the most important of all the extract additives used to improve the quality of a beer.

Lager Malts

There are major differences between the processes of lager- and beer-making, and those associated with malting are as important as those associated with fermentation and maturation. There are so many variations from country to country in lager-making that any comparison between the malts used can only be in the most general terms. Lager malts are usually far lighter in flavour than pale malts, due to the use of different varieties of barley germinating for shorter periods and kilning, usually at a lower temperature. Some brewers make a lager-type beer, often very fine, from pale malt by relying solely on the yeast and fermentation temperature to give it a lager taste. Whilst the type of yeast used can have a significant effect on the final taste it still cannot make true lager unless it has the correct material to work on. A good lager can be made from pale malts—but the best ones are made from lager malts.

Crushing Malts

Crushing malt is a skillful operation and is one of the most difficult to perform in the kitchen. The degree to which the grain is broken is extremely important. It has to be crushed enough to be able to extract all the sugars that it contains without making the grains too small. Over-crushing will tend to set the mash solid and make it virtually impossible to strain. Having tried many different methods of crushing malt, I find that the least difficult, and most successful, is to place the grains between two sheets of cloth, then push a rolling pin over the top sheet, until the malt is crushed enough. Ruined malts, poor mashes and messy kitchen floors have taught me one lesson: always buy crushed malts.

Buying Malts

Well-crushed malt consists of halves of grain, with a dry powder inside that will leave the husk relatively easily. If you crush one of the grains between your fingers and the powder does not leave the husk, then it is probably slack.

When bought, malt is usually of a good quality, but it will deteriorate quickly if stored incorrectly. Malt is manufactured at a high temperature when it is started. As the temperature drops it will naturally absorb water vapour from the air. Leave it uncovered and it will absorb moisture like a sponge and become slack. Therefore always ensure that the malt is kept in an air-tight container.

Alternatively it is possible to buy malt and hops from a brewery. Attitudes towards the sale of starting materials for home brewing varies from brewery to brewery. So do not be surprised if your request is refused. The breweries that will sell materials will probably expect you to purchase at least half a hundredweight (25 kilos) so do not approach them unless you are a relatively large-scale brewer. You may also have difficulty in persuading them to sell you ready-crushed grains. If you succeed, you will at least have the satisfaction of knowing that you are using the same materials as your competitors, but I would be surprised if you notice any difference in the quality of the beers that you brew.

Malt Extract

Malt extracts are used by some commercial brewers and only the best starting materials and methods are involved in their preparation. This does not mean that some products are not better than others, nor that you should not experiment with them by adding other ingredients and adjusting your brewing techniques. I am still convinced that handled correctly you can make beers from extracts every bit as good as those obtainable from grains.

Malt extracts are available in two types:

Diastatic Unhopped Extracts

These are made from pale malts and by careful evaporation continuing enzyme activity is assured. These may be used, along with sugar, hops and water, to make the beer, or they can be used mashed together with malts. This is the way the breweries do it. Either way you have at least part of your mashing done by professionals.

Hopped Wort Extracts

Canned beer kits are hopped wort extracts, but since they are meant to produce a beer by adding only sugar and water they may contain other ingredients (such as heading liquid). The hops are boiled with the malt in manufacturing the kits and consequently they retain no diastatic activity. Therefore it is pointless to use them in conjunction with malt, but dried malt extract and extra hops can be added to the kit to improve the quality of the beer.

Dried Malt Extract

This is made by evaporating the liquid extract until all traces of water are removed. It is safest to assume that the malt retains none of its diastatic activity and the starch will have been totally converted to sugar. Beers can be made successfully from dried malt extract with the minimum amount of work and, like crystal malt, it is a useful additive for kit beers. Dried extracts of both pale and dark malts are available.

Hops

Malt provides the beer with body and, in the case of dark ales and stouts, some of the flavour, but the vast majority of the flavour is derived from the hops. Hop produced flavours are a complex subject, but two distinct elements can be identified, bitterness and aromaticity. There is a wide variety of hops for both professional and amateur brewers to choose from. Scientific assessments of the bitterness of hops is made on the basis of the alpha acid content, which ranges from 3.0 to 10.0% of the total weight of the dried hops. Hops with high alpha acid contents seem to be the most economical, but unfortunately the acid content bears no relationship to the aromaticity. It is therefore not possible to select hops on their alpha acid range alone, (now being quoted by some suppliers). Consideration must also be given to other characteristics. The correct 'hopping rate' and the condition of the hops is more important than the specific variety.

Recommended hops for the various types of beer are given in the recipe section.

Buying Hops

The best place to buy hops is a local brewery, if they are prepared to sell them. Do not expect to select your own variety and ask for no less than a pound—they will certainly not wish to deal in smaller quantities. Many breweries blend their hops, and may well sell them already blended. If you are used to drinking their beers, you will notice that the blended hops give you a similar drink.

Few people will be able to cope with a pound of hops at a time, and therefore the best source for the average brewer is a home brew shop. Their standards are now very high. When you have decided which hops you require, buy a year's supply in January or February when the new season's crop is on sale. In assessing the quality of hops (which should always be sold in a clean plastic bag), select those which are mainly unbroken and without too much yellow dust at the bottom of the bag. The active ingredients of the hops are contained in these dust particles and they should be retained with the rest of the flower for use. Hops will deteriorate through oxidation so it is advisable to use them within a year. The speed of oxidation increases with temperature and sunlight. Dampness can result in other chemical deterioration and fungal attack. To avoid these problems always store hops in air-tight, opaque containers in a cool place. After a few months the outer hops in the container may have turned brown, but those on the inside will still be green, and since only a small fraction will have oxidised, all the hops may be used.

Do not attempt to use wild hops, through either economy or curiosity. Having tried making beer from these I have found that it takes ages to gather enough, the drying is tedious, and the final beer is terrible.

As your brewing progresses, you may like to try mixing two varieties of hops to see if blends of hops are an improvement.

Hop Oil

Commercial brewers sometimes use a hop extract called hop oil. Not only because this is convenient, but also because by controlled heating in the extraction process it is possible to drive off some of the stronger flavouring in varieties such as Bullion, which although possessing many admirable properties, tends to be overpowering when used as the sole hop. Hop oil is very concentrated and it is easy to add too much. Its main benefit to the kitchen brewer is to increase the hop aroma either in the barrel or before bottling. If you should decide to use this hop oil, add it one drop at a time from an eye dropper, tasting the liquid after each drop.

Adjuncts

Economic factors in the past have led to a search for ingredients other than malt from which beers could be made. These alternative grains are known as 'adjuncts'. Some adjuncts produce inferior beer, with clearing problems and poor taste. Others improve the quality and give a distinctive flavour to the beer. Very few adjuncts possess any enzyme activity of their own and the starch which they contain has to be converted into sugars by the excess enzymes of the pale malt. If adjuncts are used they must be included in a full mash or half-mash brew and should never be added to a kit. Since even pale malt will have only a small enzyme quantity in excess of that required to convert its own starch to maltose, no more than ten per cent of the total solids being mashed should be adjuncts.

Even such small amounts of adjuncts will be unusable if they are in a form that the enzymes cannot act upon. Many must be treated in a special way before they can be added to the mash, so only buy these ingredients if they are sold specifically for brewing. Do not use other products, however similar they may seem, since if they cannot be converted into fermentable products all you get is a hazy, undrinkable brew.

Wheat Malt

There is insufficient enzyme in wheat malt to use it entirely for brewing. I have tried several times but with little success. It affects the flavour and whether it improves it is a matter of opinion. You may like to replace 5–10% of the malt in pale ales and lagers with wheat malts.

Brewing Flour

This is a grain flour, which may be used to increase the body of a beer without increasing the malt content. There is little discernable taste and it may be used safely in any brew.

Flaked Rice

Flaked rice contributes little flavour to the beer and is used as an alternative to extra sugar. It has the advantage of providing a slight amount of additional body to beers such as lager, where the lack of added flavourings is important. You can replace up to half a pound of sugar in a five gallon brew with ten ounces of flaked rice. (Replace ½ kilo in 25 litres with 550 gm). But I would not do it myself.

Flaked Barley

This definitely changes the flavour of lagers and all pale and light ales. Personally, I rather like the taste, and you can try replacing half a pound of sugar in a five gallon brew with ten ounces of flaked barley. (Replace ½ kilo in 25 litres with 550 gm).

Flaked Maize

This has a strong natural taste but can be overpowering. You may like to try using this in sweet and oatmeal stouts, but it is better avoided.

Torrefied Barley

This is made from heating barley in red-hot sand until the expanded grains burst. It is said to improve the flavour of beers, but often factors such as malt quantities and hop types have a far greater effect. It can be incorporated in the mashes for Irish Stout and Brown ales, but is not essential.

Oatmeal

As the name implies this is essential for making oatmeal stout. There are no other occasions when we should use it.

Pearl barley, roast barley and other adjuncts have been used in brewing but to little advantage. There are uses for adjuncts in the commercial brewing process since they do improve some beers, but I am of the opinion that they are only a further complication in the kitchen and suggest you stick to our motto— KEEP IT SIMPLE.

Sugar

All alcohol in beer is derived from sugar, most of which is itself obtained from malt. Sometimes it is desirable to increase the alcohol content without producing a pronounced malt flavour. This is achieved by adding extra sugar at the wort boiling stage. Sugar is far cheaper than malt and it has found favour with price-conscious brewers. There are several different sugars that the brewer can use.

Invert Sugar

It was discovered that sucrose turned a specially-produced beam of light in one direction. When the sugar had been chemically treated, or acted upon by yeast, the light is turned in the opposite direction. The beam had been *inverted* and the resultant sugar was termed invert sugar.

One reason for using invert sugars is that they speed up the time taken to make the beer. True, fermentation will start and finish a few hours sooner, possibly even a day. But if you plan your brewing correctly you will surely not be that desperate to start a new batch.

By starting the fermentation earlier, it is said that there is less risk from infection by wild yeasts. This, again, is true, but the experience of countless brews has shown me that by adding yeast straight from the container into worts containing only malt sugars and household sugars, infections do not occur. It is only if equipment is not sterilised or the beer is left uncovered, except during the time of vigorous initial fermentation, that a diseased beer is obtained.

It is possible to invert your own granulated sugar. Simply boil together two pounds (1 kilo) of sugar, two pints (1.25 litre) of water and two teaspoonfuls of citric acid for half an hour. When the solution is cool, add two teaspoons of precipitated chalk to remove the acid which will have performed its role. The resulting solution can be used in place of two pounds of sugar in a recipe, and for those people who wish to try invert sugar it represents a considerable financial saving. However, inversion of sugar is just another needless complication in the brewing process. It is our aim to turn the kitchen into a brewery occasionally, but never into a laboratory. *It is a waste of both time and money to replace household sugar with invert sugars.*

Glucose Chips

This is an invert sugar sold and often recommended for brewing. Not only is it more expensive, but it is also necessary to use 20% more to form a fixed amount of alcohol than if granulated sugar is used. It is said by its supporters that glucose produces a better flavoured beer than household sugar. Any flavouring materials in glucose (if they exist at all) will be in such small amounts that they will be undetectable against the background of malt and hop flavourings.

Demerara

Natural brown sugars do provide a distinctive flavour and colour that improve some beers and detract from others. The flavour bestowed upon the beer is very much a personal taste and you may like to try using half demerara and half white sugar in your milds, browns and stouts. If this is successful then use entirely brown sugar for the next brew. Always ensure that you use a natural brown sugar rather than one to which artificial colourings have been added.

Syrups and Treacles

Both of these can be employed in the same way as demerara sugar but they do tend to make the beer far more expensive, both because of their cost and the need to use almost 25% more to allow for the water and less available sugar contained in them.

Sweeteners

Beers cannot be sweetened simply by adding more granulated sugar because they tend to ferment to dryness. A non-fermentable sugar or non-sugar based sweetener must be used for this purpose.

Lactose

This is a virtually non-fermentable sugar used to sweeten milk stout and some brown ales.

Saccharin

This can be used instead of lactose to sweeten beers: use at the rate of one tablet per gallon (5 litres).

Other Artificial Sweeteners

These have no advantages over saccharin and tend to be slightly more expensive.

With artificial sweeteners it is easier to control the dose by using them in tablet form rather than as liquid. Ensure that you thoroughly crush the tablets—it is easiest to grind them between two spoons—before adding them to the liquid. Add the sweeteners prior to bottling the beer.

Colouring Aids

Caramel

This is sugar that has been burnt at the surface. It provides colour and a little acceptable flavouring. It does not sweeten the beer as the unburnt sugar is fermented out in the usual way. To ensure a consistent depth of browning buy caramel rather than make it. Add two tablespoons full per gallon (5 litres), prior to commencement of fermentation. This allows you to add more during fermentation to bring to the required colour, without increasing the conditioning sugar.

Gravy Browning

Used by some brewers, and useful in

emergencies, but since the only beers that require colouring are those that are low in flavour, lacking in dark malts, any foreign tastes are readily detected. It is very much a second choice and should be added until the desired colour is obtained, at the completion of the primary fermentation.

Water

Although this is the major ingredient of beer, the role of the many dissolved salts is of far greater importance during the mashing stage than the fermentation. Unless you are mashing beer, you may feel safe using tap water. With professionally prepared worts, water treatment is just a waste of time. The treatment of waters is fully discussed on pages 52–53.

Acids

As well as occasionally being required in water treatment, small quantities of acid improve the flavours of certain beers. As with all chemicals used in brewing, ensure that they are of a standard fit for human consumption.

The only ingredients you are likely to require in your beer-making are malt extract, dried malt extract, crushed malts, one or two varieties of hops and granulated sugar. The final list will depend on how many types of beer you intend making.

Chapter 5

The Balance of Beer

You have to learn to drink and enjoy beer. It is not a taste which man naturally finds pleasant. If you think back to the first glass of beer that you drank you probably did not enjoy it and only finished the glass out of politeness. These early pints became the standard by which you judged the quality of other beers. Without realizing it, you had begun to train your palate to appreciate beers. But the palate can be re-educated to accept the beers that are available. If this were not the case then standardisation by the national breweries and the changes brought about by serving keg beers could never have been forced on the public. Only by analysing the taste of your beers, in order to decide which characteristics you relish, will you be able to enjoy the full rewards of home brewing. To begin with you will probably try to copy commercially manufactured beers, but as you become more experienced you might make others which you like better than those that are marketed.

Any recipe is just a suggestion, an attempt by someone else to formulate a beer that the general public will enjoy. Many people will be more than satisfied with the recipes and make them for years, others may well feel that they would like to alter ingredients slightly to produce a different taste. This can be done, providing that you can identify the various ingredients responsible for specific tastes and realise to what extent they can be altered.

All too often the only taste that you can detect in homemade beers is a bitter yeasty one. This is not a fault of the recipe but the result of using an inferior yeast, failing to skim the yeast from the top of the liquid during the initial fermentation, or leaving the beer over a heavy yeast deposit for too long.

If your beers suffer from this flavour, often described as 'home brew taste', then you must deal with the yeast problem before you attempt to adjust a recipe or change the kit that you use. 'Home brew taste' is probably the most common reason why people stop making their own beer.

The two ingredients responsible for the flavour of a beer are malt and hops, but both of these, depending upon the type or variety, can give rise to several different tastes. Familiarising yourself with all of them presents no problems. To refresh your memory of what constitutes a malty taste, chew two or three grains of each of the main types. Wort extracts can be used in the same way by tasting a sample on the tip of a teaspoon. Adding more malt will enhance this flavour in the beer. Tasting hopped wort extract is of little use as the flavour of the hops can be intrusive and it has little bearing on the finished beer.

Hop aromas are best assessed by taking a

flower and rubbing it between the palms of the hands before smelling it. The other main factor, bitterness, is so well known that no help is needed to detect it. Do not try chewing hops, you will regret it.

Malt

Malt contributes colour, body and sugar as well as flavour to a beer. High alcohol beers need to have a good body, a deep colour that can be either dark from the use of dark and black (chocolate) malts, or the deep rich golden amber colour produced by pale malt that no artificial colouring can ever imitate. Above all, such beers should have a full malty flavour complemented by an aromatic and bitter hopiness.

At the other end of the spectrum are the beers of lower alcohol content designed to be drunk in larger quantities. A less pronounced maltiness, a lighter hop aroma and bitterness—although some people prefer their weakest beers to be well hopped—and a far less pronounced colour are the characteristics of these ales.

Since extra hops or hop oil can be added after the initial fermentation has ceased, it is possible to assess the character of beer by its taste, and the brewer who wishes to formulate his own recipes needs only get his malt rate correct to produce the ideal beer.

Experimental Brews

To make your first experimental brew, mash a total of one pound of malt for each gallon of water that you use. Generally the minimum amount of malt is a pound per gallon (500 gm per 5 litres) and the maximum is one and half pounds per gallon (if no sugar is included), although there are exceptions, you will find that

1¼ pound (600 gm) is about right for most beers.

Pale and Bitter Ales

For pale ales use 1¼ pounds of pale malt per gallon (600 gm per 5 litres). You may also like to include a ¼ pound (125 gm per 5 litres) of crystal malt, this will not only provide sugar but will also improve the colour. Select a suitable hop, such as Goldings, and use at a rate of ½ oz per gallon (15 gm per 5 litres)—you can always increase by dry hopping later—see p.37.   Light and bitter type beers, as opposed to the fuller pale ales, can be made by using only a pound of pale malt per gallon of water (500 gm per 5 litres). From this basic brew you will be able to judge whether you have your malt quantities right. Further experimental brews may be made by adjusting within the recommended limits until you are completely satisfied. Do not adjust the malt by more than 2 oz (60 gm) in consecutive brews otherwise the difference will be too great. Until you have discovered the correct malting level do not change the hopping rate or variety. You should only alter one factor at a time, or else you will not know what is responsible for any improvement. When experimenting always record your recipes and honest comments, in order to avoid making the same mistake twice.

Brown and Mild Ales

Experimental brown ales can be made in the same way by starting with one pound of pale malt and ¼ pound of dark malt per gallon (500 gm and 125 gm per 5 litres). Milds require only ¾ pound of pale malt and ¼ pound of dark malt (360 gm and 125 gm per 5 litres). Colour is developed by addition of caramel. Use Fuggles

Characteristics of the More Popular Types of Beer

Type of Beer	Starting Gravity Range	Approximate Percentage Alcohol	Degree of Hopping
Light Ale	1.030– 1.040	2.8–4.0	Medium to high
Pale Ale (including I.P.A.)	1.040– 1.050	4.00–5.3	High to very high
Bitter	1.030– 1.050	2.8–6.3	Medium to very high
Lager	1.030– 1.045	2.8–3.8	Medium to high pronounced aromatic flavour
Sweet Stout (milk)	1.030–1.045	2.8–3.8	Low
Stout Dry (Irish)	1.040–1.055	4.0–5.8	High pronounced bitter flavour
Brown Ale	1.035– 1.040	3.4–3.8	Low
Mild	1.030– 1.040	2.8–4.0	Low
Barley Wine	1.060– 1.080	6.5–9.0	High

Alcohol levels calculated on the basis that the finishing gravity is approximately 1.007.

hops for your experimental brews. As well as adjusting the total malt, you may incorporate crystal malts in other brews, and also adjust the ratio of pale to dark malt. You can vary the recipe as much as you like provided that you always include at least 80% pale malt in your grains.

Stouts

Irish or Dry stout should be full-bodied and requires a high malting level. You can use, for your initial brew, one and a quarter pounds (600 gm) of pale malt, a quarter of a pound (125 gm) of dark malt and two ounces (60 gm) of black or chocolate malt per gallon (5 litres). Use Northern Brewer hops at ¾ ounce per gallon (20 gm per 5 litres). It is the combination of the chocolate malt and the Northern Brewer hops that gives this beer its characteristic bitter taste. An increase of either of these will, in slightly different ways, increase the bitterness.

Sweet stouts are also full-bodied beers and require a malty flavour, so start with the same quantity of pale and dark malts but add two ounces of crystal malt per gallon (60 gm per 5 litres). You should also include either 2 ounces of lactose per gallon (60 gm per 5 litres) or one saccharin tablet to provide the necessary sweetness. This can be adjusted to taste in subsequent brews. Use Fuggles hops at the rate of half an ounce per gallon (5 gm per 5 litres).

Lagers

The easiest way to make an experimental lager brew is simply to use one pound of lager malt per gallon (500 gm per 5 litres) and half an ounce (5 gm per 5 litres) of Hallertau (or Saaz) hops. Lagers are low in body and increasing the

malt seldom produces the delicate flavours that are so important in this type of beer. To improve lagers you could seek out other malt supplies, but you are more likely to succeed by looking very carefully at your techniques.

These are the most popular beers and the ones you are most likely to experiment with; if you prefer some of the rare styles of beer then follow the above advice to make your own formulations.

It is possible to produce your own recipes for beers made from malt extracts, although adjusting the weight of extract used is not practical as it is sold in tins containing an exact number of pounds or kilos. It is possible to buy larger amounts and cover the lid with plastic film to store. Due to the consistency of malt extract, it is not easy to take small quantities from a large can and you will find it much easier to increase the amount of malt by decreasing the amount of water and vice versa. By adding one less pint of water to the quantity recommended for a gallon you will be increasing the malt by approximately two ounces. One pound (500 gm) of malt extract—or malt—plus a gallon (5 litres) of water usually makes about nine pints of beer. The exact volume of beer that you make can always be adjusted to take into account the size of your container. One litre of water alters the malt extract concentration by 10%.

Experimental Brews from Diastatic Malt Extracts

Pale Ales

One pound (500 gm) diastatic malt extract, 2 ounces (60 gm) crystal malt, ¼ pound (125 gm) dried pale malt extract, one gallon (5 litres) of water . Half an ounce (15 gm) Goldings.

Bitter Ales

Use the recipe given above but add an extra two pints (1.25 litres) of water.

Brown Ales

One pound of diastatic malt extract and a ¼ pound of dark malt extract plus one gallon of water (500 gm/125 gm/5 litres of water). Plus half an ounce (15 gm) of Fuggles hops.

Mild Ales

Increase the dark malt by 50% in the above recipe for brown ales. Keep the diastatic malt extract the same and use this to make an extra two pints (1 litre) of beer.

Irish or Dry Stout

One pound of diastatic malt extract, ¼ pound of dried dark malt extract (500 gm/125 gm) and the solution obtained from boiling two ounces (60 gm) of black or chocolate malt in seven pints of water (4 litres) for twenty minutes. Plus ¾ ounce (20 gm) of Northern Brewer hops.

Sweet Stout

One pound of diastatic malt extract, ¼ pound of dried malt extract, two ounces of crystal malt (500 gm/125gm/60gm). Use two ounces of lactose (125 gm) or two saccharin tablets and ½ ounce of Fuggles hops per gallon of water (25 gm per 10 litres).

Dried Malt Extracts

Alternatively dried malt may be used entirely. Initially use the same basic formula as for liquid extract beers, but as the malt sugars are more concentrated in the dried form use only fourteen ounces for every pound suggested above (850 gm for every kilo).

When you have mastered basic brewing then you can easily adapt either the recipes given above, or the more detailed brews given in chapter 8, to make your ideal tipple. You will receive far greater satisfaction making a good beer from one of your own recipes than from one of mine.

Sugar

All the recipes formulated above rely entirely upon malt to provide the necessary sugar, which is far cheaper than malt. However far too much sugar is recommended in many recipes. It provides the beer with nothing other than alcohol and carbon dioxide. The alcohol effectively dilutes the beer, and simultaneously the body, flavouring and colouring decreases. Moreover, beers that are made with large quantities of household sugar tend to present problems with both head formation and retention.

Sugar can be used at about the rate ¼ pound to a gallon (125 gm to 5 litres). Above this amount you may produce a noticeably inferior beer. In all recipes which do not mention sugar you can replace up to 25% malt with an equal weight of sugar. Alternatively you can add ¼ pound of sugar per gallon to the standard recipes given above, if you want to make a higher alcohol beer.

The Hydrometer

It is possible to make beer without buying a hydrometer, but it is an unwise economy. You definitely need one to test when fermentation is complete, and if you want to know approximately how much alcohol your beer will contain before you make it. A hydrometer is an

HYDROMETER MAY BE CALIBRATED
TO READ 1·030 OR 30 OR 1030·
EACH REFERS TO A SPECIFIC
GRAVITY OF 1·030
(ie 1mL of the liquid weighs 1·030 gms.)

CORRECT
READING

instrument for measuring the gravity of liquid. Water has a standard gravity of 1.000 i.e. one millilitre (c.c.) of water weighs one gram. When solids dissolve in water the gravity of the water increases. The hydrometer tells us how much solid there is dissolved in the liquid. A wort will contain many different solids in solution, but only two are present in the liquid to any significant context, the fermentable sugars and the slowly fermentable carbohydrate dextrin. As fermentation proceeds, the sugars are converted into alcohol which dilutes the solution and lowers the gravity. The hydrometer is used to find out how much sugar is in the liquid before and after fermentation, and from a simple calculation it is possible to deduce the approximate amount of alcohol that will be formed.

The hydrometer is a hollow glass tube weighted at one end so that it floats upright in a liquid. In liquids that are not very dense the instrument will almost sink, with only the top of the tube above the surface, whereas with a very dense liquid virtually all of the instrument floats. The hydrometer is calibrated by marking the position at the top of the tube in a known low-density liquid and the position at the bottom of a known high-density liquid. The scale between is then divided equally to give the calibration. The specific gravity of water is 1.000 and should you damage the hydrometer you can always ensure that it is functioning correctly by checking it against water when it should record 1.000 at 60°F. To check at a different temperature apply the factor given in the temperature correction chart. To use the hydrometer, place the instrument in a hydrometer pot, (a tall glass or vase will suffice). Give it a gentle turn and read the calibration where the stem comes to rest. You will see that the liquid appears to rise up the stem of the instrument: the correct gravity is obtained by reading the level where the surface of the liquid just meets the stem.

The value that you read on the hydrometer is the true specific gravity and may, for example, be 1.046. Some brewers refer to this as a gravity of a thousand and forty six, a gravity of 1.000 is referred to as a thousand. Others refer to a gravity of 1.000 as zero and that of our example as forty six. Hydrometer calibration reflects this, and you may find that your instrument is calibrated at 1.000 as 1.000, zero, or 1000, and at 1.100 as 1.100, 100 or 1100. It does not matter which system you use, all you need to know is whether the gravity has stopped dropping and that it is safe to bottle the beer, or possibly the amount by which it has dropped to calculate the alcohol content.

Separate beer- and wine-making hydrometers may be bought but this is unnecessary as the instruments are identical in every respect except the units in which they are calibrated. If you possess a wine-making hydrometer, simply work in the units that the scale is quoted, or convert to the specific gravity.

It is often necessary to compare gravities recorded at different temperatures. For instance, if you wish to add extra materials to increase the starting gravity, you need an accurate figure and cannot ignore the temperature at which the value was recorded. The true gravity at 60°F can be found by taking the temperature of the liquid and multiplying the hydrometer reading by the value given in the chart.

The carbon dioxide generated during fermentation will increase the buoyancy of the liquid and give a false reading therefore gravities should be taken when the yeast is added. Any reading taken during the initial fermentation will be considerably higher than the true value and is at best only of interest for monitoring the

Table II: Gravity Correction Factor

Temperature

°F	°C	
45	8.5	0.96
50	11	0.97
55	13	0.98
60	15.5	1.00
65	18.5	1.01
70	21	1.02
75	24	1.04
80	26.5	1.05

OTHER temperature corrections may be calculated pro rata.

To find the true gravity multiply the figure after the decimal point by the factor then add 1.000. Example: Hydrometer reading is 1.046 at 70°F. True gravity at 60°F = 0.46 x 1.02 + 1.00 = 1.047. As you can see there is only a slight difference in the two results.

progress of fermentation.

No beers should be bottled above 1.010 and some extract beers may ferment down to 1.000. When gravity is below 1.010 and does not drop for two consecutive days it is safe to bottle the beer.

Gravity and Alcoholic Strength

The alcoholic strength is related to the starting gravity of the beer. An approximate value for the alcoholic strength can be found by multiplying the difference in starting and finishing gravity by 125. If the starting gravity was 1.046, and the final gravity was 1.006, the alcohol content would be 1.046—1.006 x 125 which is 5%. (This figure is only approximate since the true value will depend upon the efficiency of the yeast strain and the amount of oxygen and carbon dioxide present during fermentation.) If both gravity readings are taken at the same temperature or within 5°F (2.5°C) of each other there is no need to correct for temperature, but if the temperature differential is greater then correct all values to 60°F.

Although this value is only approximate it is still extremely useful in formulating recipes. The hydrometer is still used officially as the method for levying taxes so it cannot be too far out!

Apart from checking when fermentation has ceased, the other main use of the hydrometer is to increase (or decrease) the starting gravity to the level that you require. As a general rule brews with starting gravities below 1.030 produce beers that are too weak. This necessitates adding extra sugar to the weak wort. However, the excess use of sugar produces an unbalanced beer, and when you repeat the brew you will need to add extra malt or extract to avoid a repetition. Table III gives the amounts by which the major beer-making ingredients raise the gravity of beer.

Table III

Ingredient	Amount by which one pound raises the gravity of 1 gallon, or 500 gm raises the gravity of 5 litres
Pale Malt	0.028–0.030
Lager Malt	0.029–0.031
Malt Extract (Typical)	0.030
Dried Malt Extract (Black or Pale)	0.032–0.034
Sugar (White Granulated)	0.036

The amount the gravity is raised will depend upon the quality of of the malt, the method of extraction and the efficiency of the mashing. Adjuncts and brewing sugars are omitted since the percentages used are extremely small and they should not be used simply for increasing gravity.

Returning to the brew that you have prepared, for every ounce of sugar that you add to the gallon the gravity will rise by two and a quarter units (50 gm per 5 litres will raise the gravity by 3.5 units). If you wish to raise the gravity from 1.030 to 1.045 you will need to add 6 ounces of sugar per gallon. To ensure a better balance you should add to the brew either 6 ounces of dried pale malt extract, or 3 ounces each of malt extract and sugar. To increase the alcohol in the beer, again taking an average value for sugar and dried malt extract, for every 5 ounces that you add to a gallon of wort the potential alcohol rises by 1% (130 gm in 5 litres gives the same effect). When adding extra sugar or malt at this stage, dissolve it in the minimum amount of hot water, and add to the wort by stirring in.

Hops and Hopping Methods

Depending on how strong a hop flavour you want, between a half and an ounce of hops are usually added to a gallon of beer (15–30 gm to 5 litres). Given the choice, many people prefer a much hoppier beer than they can buy in the pub. Fortunately we can increase the quantity of hops by dry hopping after the initial fermentation stage when, although the beer will by no means taste its best, it is possible to ascertain if there are enough hop oils present. For this reason it is advisable not to add more than half an ounce per gallon (15 gm per 5 litres), to the boiling wort. I have tended to keep the hopping rate low in all my recipes leaving you to make your own adjustments.

Whether using malt extract or a home-mashed wort to reconstitute a wort, always bring the liquid to a rolling boil before adding the hops. This rolling boil should be maintained throughout the boiling period. As the hops boil many of the delicate flavours responsible for the aroma are volatilised off. This can be overcome to some extent by having a loosely-fitting lid on the boiling vessel. Do not fit any lid so tightly that the steam cannot escape. When making a mash beer it is important to boil for one and a half hours to ensure that the hot break occurs. It is also better to add the hops in two halves, one half at the beginning of the boil, and the remainder about a quarter of an hour before the end. Even then the beer does not always possess the true hop aroma. This can be corrected by dry hopping.

Dry Hopping

The extraction of the essential oils by dry hopping is a completely different process from boiling the hops. Boiling the water increases the solubility of water soluble compounds and is the only way of extracting them efficiently. When dry hops are added to either a partially or totally fermented beer, the alcohol present will dissolve out other compounds that are insoluble in water. By using both methods of hopping a far wider range of flavourings enter the beer: in the main those responsible for the bitterness come from boiling and those that provide the aroma come from dry hopping. Whilst using both methods together works out less efficient in terms of hops used, the vast improvement in the beer more than compensates for the increase in cost. As a general rule, boil two-thirds of the total hops with the wort and add one-third as dry hops. Once

you have decided whether you require more or less bitterness or aromaticity from the hops you can adjust the ratio accordingly.

To dry hop simply add the hops to the fermenting liquid after the initial vigorous fermentation has subsided, and leave for three to seven days before straining and bottling. Do not dry hop in a demijohn: there is not enough room for the hops to disperse.

Hop Oil

Another way to increase the hoppiness of a beer is to add hop oils. These oils, which are expensive, are so concentrated that even a slight error can result in a seriously over-hopped beer. But the advantage of using them is that they can be added at any stage, even immediately prior to bottling, and they are not as messy as hops. Hop oil should not be used as an alternative to boiling hops with the wort but only for final adjustment.

To use hop oil, add the liquid a drop at a time stirring constantly; taste the liquid after each drop. Should you add too much the taste cannot be removed.

Clarity of Beer

Cloudy beer comes from bad brewing, and if you are careful you are unlikely to experience it. Cloudiness most commonly occurs when mashing beer; hazes in extract beers are extremely rare. Do not be deterred from formulating your own recipes because you feel that the beer will be cloudy. Cloudiness can result from starch which has not completely converted to sugars. This can be rectified by testing the liquid with tincture of iodine see page 47. If starch is present, simply continue the mashing process until the starch test is negative. Proteins can cause hazes when malts are used

RACKING THE BEER

PLACE THE FERMENTING BUCKET ON THE KITCHEN SURFACE WITH A CLEAN STERILISED CONTAINER BELOW

PLACE THE END OF THE TUBE IN THE TOP BUCKET WITH THE 'U' BEND RESTING ON THE BOTTOM

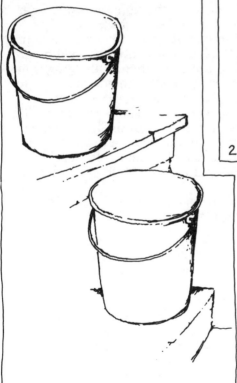

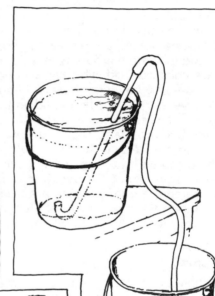

1.

2.

SUCK THE TUBE UNTIL LIQUID ENTERS THE MOUTH

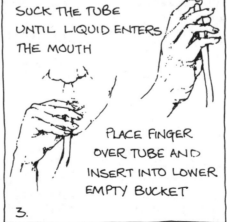

PLACE FINGER OVER TUBE AND INSERT INTO LOWER EMPTY BUCKET

3.

LIQUID WILL NOW FLOW INTO THE LOWER BUCKET

4.

whose nitrogen contents are too high but more often they occur through not boiling the wort long enough for the hot break to take place.

Cloudiness in both mashed and extract beers is also caused by suspended yeast sediment when a good beer yeast has not been used. This can be removed simply by the addition of finings. They are not otherwise necessary. I have found that if you bottle a clear beer, racked from the lees, it will contain enough live yeast cells, still in the liquid but undetectable to the naked eye, to condition the beer, but not so much that the beer deteriorates too quickly. I have several stouts, over a year old that are in their prime.

Commercial brewers usually use isinglass, the swim bladder of the sturgeon, to fine their beers. Isinglass liquid can be difficult to make up from the solid, and it is far better to buy a ready-prepared solution, even though these are slightly more expensive. It is easier to prepare a gelatine gel as sold for cooking which is equally effective in removing yeast sediments.

Never bottle a cloudy beer. Always fine it first. Should fining not clear the beer, then you can be sure that the problem is due to either starch or protein haze. This will not adversely affect the taste of the beer, so bottle and condition it in the normal way. Slightly hazy beers usually taste no different from clear beers, but it is better to drink them yourself rather than give them away as there are still some people who judge the quality of beer on the clarity. If you do make a cloudy beer, next time use a different yeast.

Racking

To separate clear beer from dead yeast cells it is necessary to rack the beer. For this you will require a racking tube consisting of a U tube and a length of plastic as described on page 3. Place the beer on the kitchen work bench with the minimum amount of disturbance, and the sterilised fermentation bucket or other container on the floor. Insert the U-tube so that the short stem of the racking tube ensures that none of the sediment is carried over with the beer. Syphon the liquid by sucking through the tube, place your finger over the end and insert the tube into a clean bucket. Discard the sediment remaining in the fermentation vessel and wash immediately, because dried yeast sediments are extremely difficult to clean.

A knowledge of the rules of balancing the various styles of beer and brewing techniques will allow you to compound your own beers and know that they will be acceptable. By continual experimentation you should arrive at an ideal and possibly unique individual brew.

Chapter 6
Making the Beer I: Malt Kits and Extracts

Kits

Probably the most popular—and certainly the easiest—method of making beer, a fact which has led to the false assumption that kits produce poor beers possessing the so-called 'home brew taste'. As has been explained previously, this is due not to the kit but to the type of yeast used and the failure to skim during fermentation. These are common mistakes of home brewers and most of them use kits, so it is easy to see how this mistake arose.

The majority of home brewers find that they can make a satisfactory standard of beer from kits, and that they need look no further. This is not to say that we cannot improve the quality, or change the character, of the beer we produce.

It is difficult to generalise about beer kits as there are so many, but two common faults are a low hopping rate and insufficient malt for the quantity of beer the kits are designed to make. To counteract the malt deficiency, the manufacturers usually give instructions to add extra sugar. The extra sugar increases the gravity and produces sufficient alcohol but a far lower quality of beer, deficient in both body and flavour, and with a poor head. This reliance on large amounts of added sugar is another reason for the belief that decent beer cannot be made from kits.

Kit manufacturers recommend this because it is cheaper for them. Realising that lack of malt is probably the biggest single fault with kit beers, some manufacturers have suggested that you add a smaller volume of water (80%) to the extract than is usual to make a better quality beer.

It is not possible to recommend brands due to the large and growing number of kits already on the market. The only indicator that you have is the amount of extract provided for each gallon of beer; even this is not conclusive as you are not aware of the degree of concentration. Ideally you need about a pound of malt extract for every gallon of beer (500 gm for every 5 litres).

Where the instructions tell you to add sugar, you may use dried malt extract which, although more expensive, greatly improves the quality of beer. Since you can use either granulated sugar or malt to provide at least a part of the added brewing sugars you must strike a balance between your palate and your pocket. By using only dried malt extract your beer will still be only a fraction of the commercial price. Many people have tried home brewing and, disappointed with the result, have gone back to buying all their ale.

This is a pity, because by paying a little more they would have been satisfied with their home brewed ales. 'Do not spoil the beer for a happorth of malt'.

Making the Beer

The only equipment required is a fermentation bucket, and possibly a demijohn, for every gallon that you are making. Although a large boiling vessel is by no means essential, it allows you to make beer by what I personally consider a better method.

When making the beer it is essential that all utensils used after the boiling stage are absolutely sterile. Not only must the malt, hops and other ingredients be completely free from airborne yeasts and bacteria, so must the equipment. Even if equipment appears to be clean it may still harbour microscopic spores, which will thrive under the same conditions as those so carefully created for the yeast. *An infected piece of equipment at any stage can spoil your beer.*

Use only stainless steel saucepans and preserving pans for boiling the worts. This process not only sterilises the wort, but also the utensils, so these do not require further treatment. All plastic and glass equipment can be sterilised by placing in a bucket with an ounce (25 gm) of sodium metabusulphate and half a teaspoonful of citric acid mixed with a pint (½ litre) of cold water; inside a fermentation bucket, which itself will be rendered germ-free in the process. Fit the lid tightly and leave standing for twenty four hours. The equipment should be washed thoroughly and is then ready for use. Care should be taken not to inhale the fumes from the sterilising mixture as they can damage the lungs.

A quicker and better method of sterilising glass and plastic is by using domestic bleach, and again great care must be taken to avoid the fumes and to ensure that the equipment is thoroughly washed after use. It is the cheapest, quickest and most efficient sterilisation available to the home brewer. Place about one fluid ounce (25 ml) of bleach and a pint of water (½ litre) in the fermenting bucket with the equipment, fit the lid and then leave for half an hour. The equipment is sterile and ready for beer-making after six or seven washings with cold water.

Your First Brew

Kit beers come complete with instructions and for your first brew it is advisable to make the beer according to the manufacturer's instructions. In a subsequent brew use the slight, but significant variations that I have suggested and decide which is the better brew. Check with the fault finder chart for improvement in future brews.

General Method for Making Kit Beers

Stage 1

Before using either a hopped or unhopped extract it is advisable to warm the thick treacle-like liquid to allow it to flow. Open the can and place it in a saucepan, which should then be filled with water to within two inches (5 cm) of the top of the can. The water should then be heated to the highest temperature possible, remembering that you have to pick up the can to pour.

Place the contents of the can in the fermenting bucket, then wash it out with about 2 pints (1.25 litre) of very hot water, together with the recommended sugar or malt extract. Add four pints (2.5 litres) of boiling or very hot water for every gallon (5 litres) of beer that the kit will make (if you have a kit that gives an alternative recipe involving less water then use the quantity recommended). Stir thoroughly to ensure that all the malt extract has dissolved. This method is quicker, involves less washing up and avoids the use of a large boiling vessel. However, you may occasionally find quantities of undissolved malt in the final beer if you are not careful. To overcome this, place all the ingredients except the yeast in the saucepan and bring to the boil. Cool to about 70°F (21°C).

Stage 2

Transfer to the fermenting bucket, adding sufficient tap water to bring it up to the premarked level on the side of the bucket—this is why it is important not to use too much water in reconstituting the wort. Water can always be added, it cannot be taken away.

Check the gravity, applying the temperature correction and add any extra sugar or water necessary to bring the gravity to the desired level as given in tables II and III.

If you wish to leave out the hydrometer and additions, then proceed straight to stage three fermentation.

These include the most likely conversion ranges and other values can be calculated pro rata—should *larger* adjustments be necessary at this stage you should use either more or less malt extract at the initial stage. Do not worry if the final gravity is still a few degrees out, where values differ from the optimum by less than 0.005 it is not likely to affect the quality of the beer.

Stage 3

Add the yeast directly to the brew and maintain at the recommended temperature.

Table IV
Sugar to be added to raise gravity

Actual Gravity	Required Gravity	Add oz sugar for every gallon of liquid	Add gms sugar for every 10 litres of liquid
1.020	1.030	4	300
1.020	1.040	8	600
1.030	1.040	4	300
1.030	1.050	8	600
1.040	1.050	4	300
1.050	1.060	4	600

Sugar may be replaced by dried pale malt extract.

Water to be added to lower gravity

Actual Gravity	Required Gravity	Water in pints to be added to 1 gallon of wort	Water in ml to be added to 10 litres of wort
1.060	1.055	1	1
	1.040	4	4
1.050	1.040	2	2
	1.030	4	4
1.040	1.030	2	2

Stage 4

Look at the beer. If after twenty-four to forty-eight hours there is no sign of activity—which at this stage may be a few tiny bubbles coming to the surface—then add a fresh sample of yeast. If no bubbles are visibly breaking the surface, listen carefully, as sometimes you can hear the bubbles when you cannot see them. Failure to start fermenting is uncommon.

By the third or fourth day there will be a large white or brown head on the beer. The head contains a gum-like substance which will also be found on the side of the fermentation bucket. Remove all the gum from both the yeast and the bucket, leaving a small quantity of clean white froth which is rich in yeast cells. Stir the beer to allow the carbon dioxide to escape from the liquid and be replaced with air. By about day six a second voluminous head of yeast will have formed. Skim again as described above.

Leave the beer to complete its fermentation. As soon as the bubbles have stopped rising, take the gravity of the beer. Sample a small quantity and if it appears to be low in hops add a quarter of an ounce of the recommended hop variety for the beer type for every gallon of beer (6 gm per 5 litres). Replace the lid. When dry hopping leave the hops in the bucket for at least three days. Irrespective of whether hops have been added, measure the gravity again. If it has not dropped proceed to stage 5. If the gravity is still dropping let it remain in the fermenting bucket until the gravity is steady. If the final gravity has dropped below 1.006 add head retention liquid or powder.

Stage 5

Rack the beer into either a sterilised container or directly into the sterilised bottles, or a barrel. Follow the instructions given on page 39.

Stage 6

Allow at least ten days, preferably longer, for the beer to mature. Beer made in this way will be very enjoyable, but there are still several variations that you can try to improve the quality. Where lack of hop character is the main problem, then you can either add hop oil, drop by drop, or prepare your own extract.

To prepare a hop extract place a pint (⅔ litre) of water in a saucepan and bring to the boil. When the water is boiling add a quarter to half an ounce (6—12 gm) of the recommended hop variety for every gallon of beer you are making. Maintain the vigorous boil for half an hour. Allow the liquid to cool, filter, then add to the extract and other ingredients in the bucket. (But remember to include it in the calculation of the total volume of liquid.)

Should the beer appear to lack colour and flavouring, then replace two ounces (60 gm) of sugar with two ounces (60 gm) of crystal malt for each gallon (5 litres) of beer being made.

Prepare the extract by boiling the crystal malt for half an hour with 1–2 pints (½–1 litre) of water. Filter the grains and add the liquid to the extract. You will probably want to add crystal malt and hops. The two may be boiled together.

To ensure that all the malt is completely dissolved, the extract, hops, crystal malt and dried malt can be placed in a saucepan with half the total water and boiled for half an hour. Filter and transfer to the fermentation bucket. Add the remainder of the water. When the temperature has dropped to 70°F (21°C) add the yeast. The quantities of malt extract, dried malt extract, sugar, hops and crystal malt can all be changed within the specified limits. In this way it is possible to make virtually any type of beer. In order to find the effect of a particular ingredient you should only alter one factor in each brew.

One of the easiest methods of improving the quality of a kit beer is to use less water than the manufacturer recommends. This technique is particularly useful if you have found the beer to be thin with a slightly acid taste. Acid, sometimes added to kits to ensure good fermentation with all waters, is readily detectable if there is

MAKING BEER FROM LIQUID

1.

INGREDIENTS AND EQUIPMENT

2.

HEAT THE CAN IN A SAUCEPAN
TO SOFTEN THE CONTENTS.

METHOD
USING A
LARGE
BOILING
VESSEL

METHOD
USING
ONLY A
PLASTIC
BUCKET

3. ADD EXTRACT, EXTRA SUGAR, ANY
EXTRA MALT AND HALF THE TOTAL
VOLUME OF WATER.
HEAT TO BOILING WITH CONSTANT
STIRRING TO ENSURE THE SUGAR
DOES NOT BURN.

3.

PLACE MALT
EXTRACT, EXTRA
SUGAR AND ANY DRIED MALT REQUIRED INTO
THE BUCKET AND SUFFICIENT WATER TO
DISSOLVE ALL THE SOLIDS COMPLETELY.

MALT EXTRACT AND KITS

4.

WHEN BOILING ADD ANY EXTRA HOPS AND CONTINUE BOILING FOR A FURTHER TWENTY MINUTES.
IF NO EXTRA HOPS ARE REQUIRED REMOVE FROM HEAT AS SOON AS THE LIQUID REACHES THE BOIL.

5. WHERE EXTRA HOPS ARE ADDED STRAIN THROUGH MUSLIN INSIDE A COLANDER INTO A FERMENTING BUCKET

6. ADD TAP WATER TO BRING THE LIQUID TO THE REQUIRED LEVEL. WHEN THE TEMPERATURE IS AT 65-70° (18·21°C) ADD THE YEAST, COVER THE CONTAINER AND MAINTAIN TEMPERATURE.

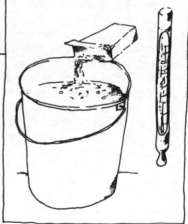

BRING 1½-2 PINTS (¾-1 litre) OF WATER TO THE BOIL. ADD EXTRA HOPS, COVER LOOSELY AND MAINTAIN VIGOROUS BOIL FOR 20-30 MINUTES.

5. STRAIN THE LIQUID FROM THE HOPS INTO THE FERMENTING BUCKET.

insufficient malt present. By making only seven pints (4.5 litres) for every recommended gallon (5 litres), the quality of the beer is vastly improved.

Do not be frightened to change the brand of kit that you use. By experimenting with the brews, beer-making becomes a far more interesting hobby. To find out how to overcome particular problems in future brews, use the fault finding chart. (See also Chapter 5: The Balance of Beer).

Making Beer from Unhopped Extracts

Unhopped malt extracts differ from their hopped counterparts in that they are not boiled with the hops, and retain most of their enzyme activity. This allows you to use them in two different ways. Firstly, in the same manner as kits, but with the advantage of knowing how much malt you have in the brew (some kits contain added sugar so that the brewer also needs to add water.) Secondly, you can also add the variety of hops that you want. Unhopped wort extracts do add an extra dimension to your brewing, and it is worth making your beer from these. Although the method differs slightly from that given for kit beers, adjustments (after the initial brew) can be made in the same way. Recipes for making beers from unhopped concentrated worts are given under the various beer types in the recipes section.

Stage 1

Mix the unhopped extract sugar and hops in about 1 gallon (5 litres) of water. Bring to the boil, stir to ensure that all soluble ingredients except the hops have dissolved. Keep it boiling as vigorously as is practical for an hour and a half. If you have experienced any difficulty in the past with the clarity of the beer, add Irish moss about half an hour before the end of the boil.

Stage 2

Pour the liquid through a strainer or piece of muslin inside a colander which has been sterilised, and make up the liquid to 1 gallon (5 litres) with tap water.

Stage 3

When the temperature has dropped to 65°F add the yeast and proceed according to the method given for kit beers.

The Half-Mash Method

The half-mash method gives you many of the advantages of mashing without the need for so much detail or expense. Whether to progress, if that is the right word, to the full mash, is a decision that you must make for yourself as the half-mash method alone can result in excellent brews.

It consists of providing half of the total malt for the beer as malt extract, and the other half as pure malt. By using the malt extract, which will possess an excess of enzymes, you are allowing yourself room for error if the mashing conditions are not perfect. However the better the mashing conditions, the better the beer will be. Should you raise the temperature too high, you will end up with a high dextrin extract, giving the beer too much body. Good body is an essential of beer, but do not overdo it.

Making the Beer by the Half Mash Method

Recipes are given under the individual types of beer but the principle is the same in all cases.

Stage 1

Raise the temperature of three pints of water for every pound of grain (3 litres for every kilo) to 160–170°F (71–77°C). Place the water in the mash tun and stir in the well-mixed grains.

Stage 2

Open the can of malt extract and place in a saucepan with warm water (not above 150°F). When the contents are soft, pour them into the mash tun together with 3 pints of water for every pound of extract, washing through any residual extract with the minimum amount of water. All water used at this stage should be raised to the mashing temperature. Adjust the temperature of the mash to 148–154°F (65–68°C) by the addition of water or any of the other recommended methods. It is possible to reverse the processes involved in stages 1 and 2 i.e. add the malt extract first, and then the grains. Both methods produce the same result, and do not affect the quality of the beer.

Stage 3

Maintain the temperature between 148–154°F for two hours, stirring to ensure that the grains do not stick to the bottom of the pan. To avoid watching the pan all the time, bring the temperature up to the maximum of the range, take the pan away from the heat, replace the lid and wrap the pan in blankets. Check the temperature every twenty minutes—reheating as necessary. Other methods of maintaining temperature, equally applicable here, are discussed under mashing.

Should you find that you have allowed the temperature to drop too low, it only means that the mashing stage will take longer. But do not be careless here because if the temperature is too low for too long, the body of the beer will decrease and there will be a loss of quality.

When taking the temperature ensure that the liquid is well stirred, and double check by varying the position of the thermometer as there may be significant differences throughout the liquid.

Stage 4

The length of time that the mashing process takes will depend both upon the exact temperature and the quantity of added grain and adjuncts. To be sure that mashing is complete, you should perform a starch test, or your beer may contain a starch haze that will never disappear. However, mashing for two hours will be sufficient in nearly all cases, and you may safely omit the chemical test.

Starch Test

Place about a teaspoonful of the wort on a white saucer and add two to three drops of tincture of iodine (3% solution of iodine in industrial methylated spirit, a solution obtainable from any chemist's shop). The iodine wort mixture becomes blue-black in colour if any unconverted starch remains. If this happens it is necessary to continue the mashing process further. Maintain the temperature at 150°F for a further quarter of an hour and test again. When the test for starch is negative, the wort iodine solution will be colourless or light brown due to the dilution of iodine. When this stage is reached proceed to stage 5.

Stage 5

Allow to cool, then strain the wort through either a beer strainer or a colander lined with a piece of muslin, into a vessel large enough to hold the total volume of beer that you wish to make. This container must be clean, but as the wort is going to be boiled it is not necessary to sterilise it. Sparge the grains by washing with two pints (1 litre) of water at approximately 150°F. The easiest method of sparging is to pour the water from a kettle evenly on to the grains. Allow the water to trickle from the kettle and ensure that all the grains are thoroughly washed.

Stage 6

Transfer the strained wort to a boiling pan if you are not using the same vessel for boiling and mashing. Add any additional sugar, dissolved in a pint to a quart of water and make up to the total volume. Add the hops. Boil for an hour partially covered. Mashed beers clear far better if they are shock cooled after the hops boil. The simplest way to do this is to place the boiling pan when it has cooled enough to handle, in a sink containing about six inches (15 cm) of cold water.

Stage 7

Up to this stage there is no danger of the wort becoming infected, since any germs will have been killed in the boiling process. Once the wort comes off the boil and until the beer is drunk, it is open to attack by organisms. Therefore the beer must be kept covered and all utensils which come into contact with it must be sterile. Sterilise the strainer by boiling in water, and the fermentation bucket with bleach, as described under Kit Beers.

Strain the hopped wort into the fermentation bucket, add tap water to make the volume up to required level and cover with a tightly fitting lid.

Stage 8

Add the yeast straight from the packet. Check after 24 hours to ensure that the wort has started fermenting. If there is no sign of activity, add a fresh yeast sample.

Stage 9

After the voluminous head has subsided, rack and check the activity daily. Half-mashed beers tend to have better head-forming and retaining characteristics than brews made entirely from malt extract. Do not add heading powder to your first brew. If you're not satisfied with the head, then next time add a heading compound after this stage.

You may dry hop now, if you wish, by adding a quarter of an ounce of hops to 1 gallon (7 gm per 5 litres). Leave the hops in the beer for at least three days.

When fermentation appears to have ceased check the gravity. When there is no further drop in gravity, bottle and prime by adding exactly half a teaspoonful of sugar per pint. Leave to mature and drink.

Adjustments can be made to half-mash method recipes, providing that at least half the malt is extract. Although malt is wet, for purposes of calculation assume that one pound of extract (wet basis) is equivalent to one pound of pure crushed malt. This is fairly accurate, as the insoluble materials such as husk approximately equal the water in the extract.

Another variation on the half mash method is to make a wort from either a kit or diastatic malt extract and a second wort by the full mash method and combine the two prior to fermentation. I feel that it is far easier to make all of the beer by the full mash.

Yet another method of using malt extracts is to add an equal quantity of extract to a kit beer and double the quantity of water used. This can be a very successful method of making beers, and an easy way of adding extra malt to a kit. To make beers by this method add the malt extract and kit together, incorporating the extract obtained from boiling the extra hops necessary in water and straining. Make beer by the method given for kit beers.

Dried Malt Extract

Beers made from dried malt extract possess all the advantages and disadvantages of liquid malt. It is possible to buy kits that provide dried malt extract, with or without the addition of other materials such as crystal malt. It is also possible to buy the dried malt separately, so the two variations may be considered together. Place the ingredients, except the hops and yeast in a saucepan with the water, add the hops when the liquid reaches the boil, and boil for one and a half hours. Strain the liquid into the fermenting bucket and make up to the total volume with tap water.

Then proceed by the method given for liquid extract beers or for concentrated wort extract. Since the reconstructed wort will have been made by the same basic principles all operations will be identical. Adjustments can be made for both in the same way and the same fault finder chart should be consulted.

KIT BEER FAULT FINDER

PROBLEM	SOLUTION
Cloudy beer	Add gelatine or isinglass finings. Use a different yeast for future brews
Vinegar or other off-flavours	Throw away the beer! Thoroughly sterilise all equipment and keep all air away from future brews
Over or under gassed beer	Check that fermentation has ceased with a hydrometer and add EXACTLY ½ teaspoon of priming sugar per pint (½ litre) of beer
Lack of maltiness or body	Either add 1 oz dried malt extract per gallon (300 gm per 5 litre) or add seven pints (4½ litres) of water for every gallon (5 litres) recommended in the recipe or both
Lack of Bitterness	Boil up ¼ oz (8 gms) of hops in two pints (1 litre) of water for every gallon (5 litres) of beer
Lack of Aromaticity	Dry hop with ¼ oz per gallon (8 gm/5 litres) of beer
Lack of flavour	Replace half the added sugar with crystal malt
Insufficient alcohol	Add up to ¼ oz sugar per gallon (8 gms/5 litres)
Insufficient head or head retained for too short a period	Add heading liquid

Chapter 7

Making the Beer II: Mashing

Mashing is the enthusiast's method of brewing, requiring more expensive equipment, taking more time, but above all requiring a greater degree of skill and knowledge than other methods. The quality of mashed beers cannot be denied, and whether or not a similar quality can be obtained with less effort by using kit beers and malt extract is debatable, but I believe it can. Well-mashed beers, made from good ingredients to a balanced recipe, have a superb flavour, body and depth with few head retention problems. Whether mashing is the method for you depends upon how much time you are prepared to spend on making the beer, and whether you are prepared to pay the attention to detail that is necessary. If you are willing to make the extra effort and to study the technique, then there is no reason why you should not make some really superb beers.

It is necessary to offer a word of caution. Commercial beers are made by the mashing technique, but the brewer's methods have evolved over many years and due to the many variables, of malt quality and crushed hops, operating conditions and local water supply, it is unlikely that the amateur will be able to mash without have some disappointments at the beginning. Nevertheless if you study the theory and follow the instructions carefully even your first mashed beer should be enjoyable, and again with only a little experimentation you should soon be able to brew any beer that you wish.

Equipment

As with all types of brewing, you may already possess sufficient equipment in your kitchen to allow you to conduct your first few batches without buying any special apparatus. However it is essential to have a vessel large enough to boil the volume of liquid for the beer you wish to make. In most cases this will restrict the brewer to two gallon batches, although this should be ample for experimental brews. Remember to use only stainless steel boilers. If you do decide to continue mashing, then sooner or later you will need to buy a boiler.

Water

Care is required in all aspects of mashing beers, but the mash itself—the stage at which the sugar is extracted from the grain—can present the most problems. Not only is it necessary to ensure that the mash is conducted at the correct temperature, but some attention needs to be paid to the brewing water also. Although in the commercial process no effort is spared to obtain the ideal water composition, there is no reason why in the early stages you should not forget about this aspect. But the quality of beer is improved by treating the water in certain circumstances.

It is incorrectly thought that the water itself imparts a taste to the beer. The enzymes converting the starch to sugar also react with other chemicals present in the water. Any change in taste due to the water is usually insignificant compared to that produced by the minute amounts of dissolved solids reacting with the enzymes.

These reactions will be dependent upon the type of malt used, and since it is necessary to dissolve out different materials to make the range of beers, different waters are used for different beers.

For years water has been classified according to its hardness, which is the degree of difficulty that a standard quantity of water has in forming a lather with soap solution. Hardness is further sub-divided into two types, temporary hardness, which can be removed simply by boiling the water, and permanent hardness which is unaffected by boiling.

All water originates as rainfall on the land. This dissolves out minute quantities of minerals from the ground while draining to reservoirs or rivers. The composition of the water will depend upon the nature of the terrain, and will differ considerably between areas. Some materials dissolved out in water, such as sodium chloride, have no effect on a soap solution, and although they increase the total dissolved solids they have no effect on the hardness of the water. In general, hard waters contain more dissolved solids than soft, but the most important difference is that hard waters are high in calcium and magnesium salts, important in the brewing of pale ales. Soft waters contain some dissolved solids often including sodium chloride, but if this is absent it must be added for making dark ales. Absolutely pure water, such as distilled water or rainfall is not suitable for brewing without the addition of either salt or chalk, depending upon the type of beer that you wish to make.

The source of most domestic water supplies does not usually change, and although there may be slight variations in the composition these have an insignificant effect on your brewing operations. You can ask the local water authority for an analysis of your water, but all you really need to know is whether you have hard or soft water. Hard water originates from chalkland, whereas soft water is often associated with peat lowlands. The vast majority of waters are somewhere in between. For purpose of beer-making we will define hard waters as those containing in excess of 200 parts per million total dissolved solids as calcium salts. Values below this figure are defined as soft.

Pale Ales (including light ales, bitters, Indian pale ales and barley wines)

These require a high degree of permanent hardness. If you have soft water add half a teaspoonful of magnesium sulphate (Epsom salts) and the same quantity of calcium sulphate (gypsum) to the gallon (5 litres). Burton-on-Trent, famous for centuries for the brewing of pale ales, has water that is high in both gypsum and chalk and this treatment is often referred to as 'Burtonising' the water.

Where the water is hard this treatment is unnecessary.

Dark Ales and Stouts

London is one of the great dark brewing centres

of the world and it is London water that the home brewer tries to copy when making his dark beers.

If you possess hard water then the temporary hardness should be removed by boiling for half an hour before you require it. A chalk precipitate will be seen to settle at the bottom of the container. Rack the water from the sediment which should then be discarded. Treat only enough water for the mashing and sparging stages (usually about half the total brewing water).

To make dark ales the enzymes that are active during the mash require a relatively higher level of chlorides, so, whether the water has been artifically softened by boiling or is naturally soft, always add ½ teaspoon of table salt to each gallon used for mashing. Even if the water already possesses a fairly high salt level, further additions should not be detectable in the final beer providing you add salt to the mashing liquid only and not the total brewing water.

Hard water has a lower acidity than soft water as some of the chemicals present buffer the effect of the acid. Boiling the water precipitates some of these naturalising agents out of solution. The water on cooling absorbs the acid gas carbon dioxide and the acid level is raised. With very hard water, especially if the permanent hardness is high, treat the water with lactic or citric acid in the same way as for lager (see below). Generally the extra acid will not be required, but as with lager the slight excess will cause no problems.

Lagers

As with other aspects of lager-making, the water requirements are different from those of other beers. Lager requires a higher degree of acidity than pale or dark ales at all stages from mashing to maturation. If your water is very hard then boil as for dark ales, but do not add any sodium chloride (salt). Instead add ½ teaspoonful of lactic or citric acid per gallon (5 litres) to every gallon used in the brewing operation.

With slightly hard water (150–200 ppm calcium salts) add the acid but omit the boiling treatment.

Soft waters generally require no treatment for lager brewing, except perhaps for the addition of ½ teaspoonful per gallon of acid, but this is not essential.

Special water treatment chemicals are sold by most home brew centres. If you feel that adjustments are necessary to your water supply, then use these according to the manufacturer's instructions. Your local shop will probably be able to give you information on treating your water to make all types of beer.

The Mashing Process

Before adding the grains and any adjuncts to the water, it is essential that they are well mixed. For the enzymes liberated by the pale malt to convert all the starch to sugar, they must be in the vicinity of the starch. Whilst in a liquid medium the enzymes are capable of dispersal, it would be wrong to think that they will quickly distribute themselves throughout the brew. Quick affective conversion will only occur if the grains are thoroughly mixed.

It is essential to have the mashing medium at the right consistency—I did warn you that you have to pay a great deal of attention to detail with this method! Allow three pints of brewing water for every pound of solid (3½ litres for each kilo) and bring this up to a temperature of 170°F (77°C). This is termed the 'striking temperature'.

The grains can be added to cold or warm water and gradually brought up to the mashing temperature. However this can be time consuming as great care must be taken to ensure that the mixture is not heated above the mashing temperature or that any hot spots develop. It is best to add the grains to hot water rather than cold, then adjust to the mashing temperature. Add the grains to the liquid, stirring continually as your pour. As the grains are much colder than the liquid the temperature will drop, but it is important to ensure that the grains are not at the elevated temperature for too long. If the temperature, measured in different parts of the mash, is below the quoted figure of about 150°F (62°C) then add extra hot water, with continuous stirring, until it is within 2°F (1°C) of the quoted figure. This temperature must be maintained over a period of two hours or more, to within 5°F(2.5°C). If the temperature drops below this the beer will be acceptable but will probably lack body. There are several ways of maintaining the temperature.

If you have a gas stove return the boiler to the stove when the temperature has dropped by about two to three degrees and reheat to the correct temperature or a degree or two above. Constant stirring ensures that no grains stick to the bottom of the vessel. Switch off the gas and wrap the boiler in blankets to minimise the heat losses. Check the temperature again after twenty minutes. Reheat as necessary. You will soon discover how frequently it is necessary to repeat the operation. Alternatively, leave the boiler standing on the stove uncovered, but it will require more frequent attention.

This method is not practical with an electric stove because the ring takes too long to heat up and will use too much electricity. With an electric stove adjust the heat by boiling a kettle of water, allowing it to come off the boil and adding some of it to bring up the temperature of the mash. It

is important that this water is well above the mashing temperature so that too much water does not have to be added—the consistency of the mash is important. When you add the water, stir vigorously to ensure that there are no local hot spots, as these will destroy the enzymes. Again cover with blankets to minimise heat loss.

The third method is the easiest once the equipment has been made. Make a hot box with sufficient space to hold the mash boiler and insulate thoroughly. Any box large enough will do for this purpose. Line with polystyrene as with fermentation cabinets, lined in turn with a layer of baking foil. If the boiler is placed in this box and covered with a similarly insulated lid, it will lose heat very slowly, and can be left overnight in the hot box. When you remove it the following morning you will have a perfect mash without any danger of a starch haze.

The easiest of all methods of mashing is using a Bruheat bucket. These have variable thermostats, and you can perform all the brewing operations from mashing to fermentation in the same vessel.

Whilst the correct mashing temperature is very important in obtaining a good mash, for the best result the 'floating tun' technique should be used to ensure that the liquor has free access to the grain. The best commercially available systems have a false bottom, which may be difficult to arrange with improvised equipment. To overcome this make a stout bag that can be suspended from the top of the tun. Place the grains in the bag and suspend it so that there is about an inch (2.5cm) of space at the bottom of the container. Put all the solids in the bag, then, instead of stirring the grains when you add them to the liquid, simply swirl the bag.

Usually home mashing takes about two hours to complete, although with perfect conditions it can be quicker. To ascertain that mashing is complete perform a starch test (see page 47). Do not be tempted to omit the test until you have made that particular type of beer a few times and know how long it takes, otherwise you risk having a permanent starch haze.

When the mashing stage is finished the sweet wort must be separated from the spent grains. If the grains are free in the tun, strain the liquid into a large container. The strainer must be capable of withstanding quite a weight during the sparging process, so make sure that both it and its support are strong. One way of supporting the strainer is with two stout pieces of wood across the top of the vessel into which the liquid is being poured.

Some mashing vessels contain a tap at the bottom through which the liquid can be strained. Providing the false bottom retains the majority of the grains there is no need to filter. Some particles are unavoidable, what you do not want is a large quantity of solids in the liquid at the boiling stage.

Where the grains have been held in a bag, depending upon the material that it is made from, it may not be necessary to strain the liquid, but if in doubt do so.

Sparging

Now you have less than half of the total liquid in the finished beer. Bring the balance of the water up to the mashing temperature. The temperature is not as critical as during the mash itself, but you should try to get within 5°F (2.5°C). If on heating all the solids have not been transferred from the tun to the filter bed, wash them through with this water. Never use cold water. Ideally the water used for sparging should also have the same chemical constituents. Any additions of acid, chalk, gypsum or salt are recommended for both the mashing and sparging water, and the same goes for any softening liquid.

The easiest way to sparge is to use a kettle or other utensil fitted with a spout. Pour the hot liquid slowly and evenly over the bed, making sure that the outside as well as the middle is sparged. Pour at the rate at which water can escape from the bed, otherwise the pressure that is developed when the liquid overflows the solid may force the smaller particles into the mash of the sieve and block it.

Taste the sparge liquor occasionally. Initially it will be very sweet and sticky. When there is no longer a pronounced sweet taste stop sparging — over-sparging can result in more starch being dissolved out than the remaining enzymes can handle and a haze will form. Occasionally the liquid is still slightly sweet after all the sparging water has been used up, this occurs particularly with high gravity beers. Should this happen do not heat up extra water, but discard the partially spent grains.

Make the volume of the liquid up to the recipe volume with tap water (there is no need to treat the water after the sparging process).

Boiling the Wort

Where necessary, transfer the wort to the boiling vessel. If the recipe calls for additional sugar it can be added at this stage, or after a gravity check prior to the commencement of fermentation. Where sugar is added prior to boiling, it should either be dissolved in a minimum amount of water or stirred constantly to ensure that it does not stick to the bottom of the vessel and caramelise.

Add either all the hops that you intend using or two-thirds if you intend dry hopping, then boil for an hour and a half. When boiling partially cover the vessel to stop excess evaporation and loss of aroma from the hops. With the lighter ales and lager where the aromatics are as important as the bitterness in the beer, one way to avoid dry hopping is to keep back about a half of the hops and add these 15–20 minutes before the end of the boil.

Do not be tempted to decrease the boiling time, for the governing factor is the time that it is necessary for the hot break to occur. The hot break results in protein-like material being coagulated and precipitated out of solution. If your boiling period is too short you will get a hazy beer. With all lightly coloured ales it is advisable to add Irish moss to help clarification about half to three quarters of an hour before the end of the boil. This is not so important with darker ales where the colour tends to disguise any haze. Prepare the Irish moss by making it first into a paste and then into a slurry before adding to the liquid.

Cooling the Hopped Wort

A second clarification process, the cold break, occurs naturally if the liquid is rapidly cooled. The cold break is as important as any operation in mashing and it is pointless ensuring ideal water and mashing temperatures unless you shock cool the liquid after boiling, because failure to do this will result in a hazy beer. Allow the boiling vessel to cool enough for you to handle, then plunge it into a sink, bath or other large container of cold water. Immediately the liquid comes off the boil it is open to attack by micro-organisms, therefore all utensils used after this stage must be sterilised and the beer should be kept covered.

Filtering

One operation that cannot be performed with the liquid covered is filtering. The hops and the precipitates of the hot and cold breaks are best filtered through a piece of muslin placed inside a colander both of which should have been previously boiled. Filter directly into the fermentation bucket.

Due to evaporation while boiling, the wort will have less volume than specified in the recipe. Make the level up to the mark on the side of the bucket with tap water. Check that the temperature is between 65–70°F (18–21°C) and add the yeast.

Summary of the Mashing Process

The complex mashing process can be summarised as follows:

Stage 1:   Thoroughly mix the grain and prepare the brewing water.
Stage 2:   Place the water in the mashing tun and heat to the striking temperature.
Stage 3:   Add the grain to the mashing liquor and maintain temperature until the starch iodine test is negative.
Stage 4:   Filter and sparge.
Stage 5:   Add hops and boil, treat with Irish moss if making a lighter ale
Stage 6:   Shock cool, filter and make up to the total volume with tap water
Stage 7:   Add the yeast.

When the mashed wort has been prepared, the liquid is filtered in the same manner as described for extract beers. The temperature is maintained at 65–70°F (18–21°C) or 60°F (15.5°C) for a lager. Check that the fermentation has started within 24–48 hours. If not, add a fresh yeast sample.

Three to four days after adding the yeast

MASHING BEER

1. THOROUGHLY MIX THE GRAINS

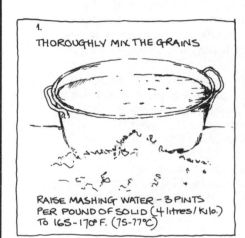

RAISE MASHING WATER – 3 PINTS PER POUND OF SOLID (4 litres/kilo.) TO 165-170° F. (75-77°C)

2. ADD GRAINS WHILST STIRRING TO THE MASHING LIQUID, OR PUT IN A BAG AND SWIRL

TAKE TEMPERATURE

3. MAINTAIN AT THE RECOMMENDED TEMPERATURE BY ONE OF THE GIVEN METHODS FOR TWO HOURS

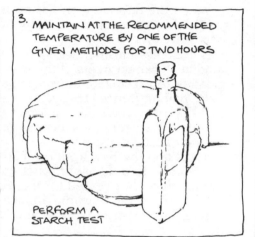

PERFORM A STARCH TEST

4. STRAIN AND SPARGE

5. ADD ANY SUGAR, BRING LIQUID TO BOIL AND ADD HOPS

6. PLUNGE INTO SINK OR BATH OF COLD WATER TO SHOCK COOL

STRAIN INTO FERMENTING VESSEL MAKE UP TO REQUIRED VOLUME, WHEN TEMPERATURE HAS REACHED 65-70° F. (20-21°C), ADD YEAST.

remove most, but not all, of the voluminous head and all of the gum-like substance on the surface and around the edge of the bucket. Repeat the operation three or four days later.

When the fermentation has finished you may if you wish taste a sample and dry hop if necessary.

Sometimes mashed beers do not clear as readily as extract beers. If the beer is cloudy add gelatine to precipitate the suspended solids. Take half an ounce (15 gm) of gelatine and add to a cup of cold water. Leave to stand for fifteen minutes. Transfer to a saucepan and warm until the gel is totally dissolved.

To obtain the best from mashed beers, rack the liquid into a demijohn when the initial fermentation has ceased (or three days later if dry hopping). Fill to within an inch (2.5 cm) of where the rubber bung rests and fit an airlock.

Under these conditions the beer will be safe for a considerable period of time. Check the gravity after a week and then regularly until fermentation has ceased. The beer should be primed and placed in either a bottle or barrel.

It is as difficult to decide on the correct recipe to suit your palate with mashed beers as with extract beers.

Mashing does not remove the need to adjust ingredients to get the perfect beer, nor is it the answer for anyone looking for an instant total success with his brewing, but for anyone prepared to spend the extra time it does add an extra dimension to the hobby.

As with all methods of brewing, faults are possible. Consult the mashed beers fault-finder chart to help identify and cure any problems that arise.

MASHED BEER FAULT FINDER

PROBLEM	SOLUTION
Hazy or cloudy beer	Treat with isinglass or gelatine finings. If beer clears try oher yeast for future brews and/or incorporate finings as standard procedure
	IF BEER DOES NOT CLEAR TRY THE FOLLOWING IN ORDER
	Perform starch test and carry on mashing until the result shows negative. Check sparged liquor to ensure starch is not going to the boiler
	If not already using Irish Moss add to the boil
	You have a protein haze. Boil for half an hour longer to ensure a good hot break. Cool quicker to ensure a good cold break
Vinegar or other off flavours	Throw the beer away! Thoroughly sterilise all equipment and keep air away from all future brews
Over or under gassed beer	Check that fermentation has ceased with an hydrometer and add EXACTLY ½ teaspoon of priming sugar per pint (½ litre) of beer
Poor extraction Gravity below 0.025 for each pound of malt per gallon	Increase mashing period or seek other malt supply
Low malt flavour or poor body	Increase pale malt by 2–4 oz per gallon (60–120 gm/5 litres)
Lack of aromaticity	Add ⅓ of the total hops twenty minutes before the end of the boil or dry hop with the same quantity of hops
Insufficient head or head retained for too short period	Add heading liquid

Chapter 8
Recipes

Light Ales

These beers are low in alcohol, malt and hops. They are thirst quenchers, designed to be drunk in larger amounts than pale ales and should be made in the summer to be enjoyed as a reward after a day's gardening.

Water Light ales need a water relatively high in gypsum and epsom salts. If you live in a soft water district add water treatment for light, pale or bitter ales when mashing the ingredients. Water treatment is not necessary when using other brewing methods.

Hops Goldings hops are the best although (as with all beers) Fuggles may be used.

Maturation Being low in the major beer components, light ales are ready for drinking far quicker than most. Ideally they should be drunk a month after you start the brew. They seldom keep for longer than three months.

Kit light ales (1)

One 2 gallon (10 litres) light ale kit
Sugar as given in the kit instructions
4 oz (100 gm) crystal malt
½ oz (15 gm) Goldings or Fuggles hops
Top fermenting yeast
Water to two gallons (10 litres)

Place the crystal malt in 2 pints (1 litre) of water in a saucepan, and bring to the boil. Place the hops in the water when it has boiled and boil for a further 20 to 30 minutes.

Meanwhile, empty the can into the fermenting bucket, taking care to wash any remaining material from the sides with hot water. Add four pints (2½ litres) of boiling or nearly boiling water to the extract and stir thoroughly to dissolve it. After the recommended boiling time, strain the water from the saucepan into the fermentation bucket. Make up to the two gallon (10 litres) mark with cold tap water. Allow to cool and when the temperature has reached 65—70°F (18.5°C) add the yeast and ferment. After the vigorous fermentation has subsided taste a small quantity to ensure that there are sufficient hops present.

Kit light ales (2)

One 2 gallon (10 litre) light ale kit
Half the sugar given in the kit instructions
A quantity of dried pale malt extract equal to the sugar used
½ oz (15 gm) Goldings or Fuggles hops
¼ oz (7 gm) optional extra for dry hopping
Top fermenting yeast
Water to two gallons (10 litres)

Place the malt extract from the kit, and the dried malt extract, in the bucket. Add six pints (3 litres) of very hot water to dissolve the malt. Boil the hops for half an hour in one pint of water in a saucepan and then strain the liquid onto the solution of malt extract. Make up to two gallons with water straight from the tap. Ferment as described and dry hop if necessary.

From liquid malt extract

2 lb (1 kilo) malt extract
12 oz (360 gm) sugar
1½ oz (45 gm) Goldings or Fuggles hops
Top fermenting yeast
Heading liquid
Water to three gallons (15 litres)

Place the malt extract and the washings from the can together with the sugar in a bucket and add six pints of boiling water. Boil the hops for one and a half hours in a pint of water and add to the liquid in the bucket. Make up to 3 gallons (15 litres) with water straight from the tap. Alternatively you can boil all of the ingredients together and if you experience any difficulties in clearing the beer, add Irish moss to the boil. Ferment in the usual way.

From dried malt extract

1¾ lb (850 gm) dried pale malt extract
6 oz (180 gm) sugar
6 oz (180 gm) crystal malt
1¼ oz (40 gm) Goldings or Fuggles hops
Heading liquid
Top fermenting yeast
Water to three gallons (15 litres)

Bring the crystal malt to the boil in two pints (1 litre) of water and then add the hops. Boil for 20–30 minutes. Strain the liquid from the boil on to the dried malt and sugar. Add a further four

pints (2½ litres) of boiling water and stir thoroughly to dissolve. If the solids do not dissolve add further boiling water (this should not be necessary). Add cold water and ferment by the general method. Dry hop if necessary. Again you may boil the ingredients together for half an hour to produce the wort.

By mashing

2 lb (1 kilo) crushed pale malt
½ lb (250 gm) sugar
¾ oz (20 gm) Goldings or other bitter hops
Top fermenting yeast
Water to two gallons (10 litres)

Bring one gallon (5 litres) of water to 165°F (68°C) and add the malt, stirring rapidly. When the malt has been added check the temperature. If it is between 148–152°F (65–68°C) maintain this temperature for at least two hours by the prescribed methods. If the temperature is outside the range, adjust by adding hot, but not boiling water or cold water. Strain and sparge the liquid and make up to as near two gallons (10 litres) as your equipment will allow. Add the hops and sugar. Boil for 1½ to 2 hours. Cool rapidly and strain. When the temperature is at 65–70°F add the yeast.

Quality mash

This is more expensive light ale than the previous recipe, but it has that extra quality which only comes from extra ingredients.

2¼ lb (1 kilo) crushed pale malt
4 oz (100 gm) crystal malt
4 oz (100 gm) sugar
Irish moss
1½ oz (45 gm) Goldings or other bitter hops
Top fermenting yeast
Water to two gallons (10 litres)

Heat seven pints (4⅓ litres) of water to 170°F (77°C) then add both the crushed and crystal malt, stirring to ensure an even distribution of heat so that the enzymes do not suffer thermal shock. Adjust the temperature to 148–152°F (55–63°C) and maintain for at least two hours.

Strain and sparge, transfer to the boiling vessel and make up to as near two gallons (10 litres) as possible. Add the sugar and hops and boil for 1½ to 2 hours. Add the Irish moss half an hour before the completion of the boil. Cool as quickly as possible then strain. Make the volume up to two gallons (10 litres). When the temperature is at 65–70°F (18.5–21°C) add the yeast. Ferment and dry hop if necessary by the prescribed method.

Mashing with adjuncts

1½ lbs (750 gm) crushed pale malt
8 oz (250 gm) flaked maize
8 oz (250 gm) sugar
1 oz (30 gm) Goldings or Fuggles hops
Irish moss
Top fermenting yeast
water to two gallons (10 litres)

Mash according to the method given in quality mash. But first ensure that the flaked maize is thoroughly mixed with the crushed malt.

By comparing the beer with that obtained from recipes for dried malt extract, mashing, quality mash or mashing with adjuncts, you will be able to see the effect of adding extra malt and flaked maize. Try each and decide which suits your palate best. Then you can create your ideal recipe. Vary the above recipes by replacing the flaked maize with flaked rice or by adding 8 oz (250 gm) of crystal malt which creates a superb light ale very similar to a pale ale.

Pale Ales

Pale ales could be described as top quality light ales. They are maltier with a more pronounced hop flavour and have a higher alcohol content than light ales. Consequently they are designed to be drunk in smaller quantities than light ales. They also tend to be more expensive to make, but you can economise by replacing some malt with sugar. However, this produces alcohol at the expense of quality, so if you prefer a cheaper brew then stick to light ales.

Water—All beers of this type need water which is high in gypsum and Epsom salts. If you do not live in an area with relatively hard water, add the water treatment for light, pale and bitter ales. Do not treat the water unless you are mashing or half mashing.

Hops—Styrian Goldings, East Kent Goldings or Fuggles hops are recommended.

Maturation—These take longer to mature than light ales and it is advisable to wait three months before drinking the beer.

Kit pale ale

For a top quality pale ale it is essential that you buy a kit that provides a relatively large amount of malt. There are kits which produce a satisfactory beer if made according to the instructions, others require slight adjustment.

two gallons (10 litres) malt extract kit
4 oz (125 gm) crystal malt
4 oz (125 gm) dried pale malt extract
8 oz (250 gm) sugar
1 oz (30 gm) Goldings or Fuggles hops
Heading liquid or powder
Top fermenting yeast
Water to two gallons (10 litres)

Place the malt extract, the crystal malt, and dried malt into a large saucepan or preserving pan together with 1–2 gallons (5–10 litres) of water.

Bring to the boil, add the hops and maintain the boil for twenty minutes. Strain into the fermenting bucket. Wash the spent crystal malt grains with hot water. Make up to two gallons with cold water.

When the temperature has dropped to 65–70°F (18.5–21°C) add the yeast and ferment in the usual way. When the initial fermentation ceases add the heading liquid. When bottling it is advisable to bottle some half pints as well as pints since this is a strong beer.

If you use a good beer kit, this method produces probably the finest of all pale ales.

Kit beers—no boiling method

This requires slightly less ingredients and can produce a beer as good as that made by the above method. It is a useful variation if you only have a small boiling vessel.

Two gallon (10 litres) malt extract kit
3 oz (90 gm) dried malt extract
6 oz (180 gm) sugar
½ oz (15 gm) Goldings or Fuggles hops
Top fermenting yeast
Heading liquid
Water to 14 pints (9 litres)

Place the malt extract and the dried malt extract with the sugar in the fermentation bucket. Cover with a gallon of boiling water and stir thoroughly until the malt has completely dissolved. Make up to fourteen pints (9 litres) with cold water. When the temperature has reached 65–70°F (18.5–21°C) add the yeast and ferment in the usual manner.

After primary fermentation has ceased add the heading liquid and hops. Leave the hops in the liquid until ready for bottling. Rack and bottle.

Half-mash

You will need a boiler capable of holding 4 gallons (20 litres) of liquid for this recipe. It is not practical to make a smaller quantity due to the size of the extract cans.

2 lb (1 kilo) diastatic malt extract
3 lb (1½ kilo) crushed pale malt
3 oz (90 gm) hops
Top fermenting yeast
Water treatment for pale beer if necessary
Water to four gallons (20 litres)

Bring two gallons (10 litres) of water up to 160–165°F (71–74°C). Add the crushed malt and then the malt extract, stirring constantly to ensure that none sticks to the bottom of the heater. Check the liquid's temperature in three or four different places in the boiler. Adjust temperature with hot, not boiling, water. Maintain the temperature at 150°F ± 2° (65°C) for two hours. Perform an iodine test after this period if you wish: this should not be necessary. Strain the liquid through a colander lined with muslin (clean but not necessarily sterilised) into the boiling vessel. Sparge with a gallon (5 litres) of water at about 150°F (65°C). Add the hops and continue boiling for 1½ or 2 hours. Cool rapidly. Strain through a sterilised colander and muslin. Make up to four gallons (20 litres) and when the temperature is at 65–70°F (18.5–21°C) add the yeast. Ferment in the usual way.

Dried malt extract–to make two gallons (10 litres)

2 lb (1 kilo) pale dried malt extract
6 oz (180 gm) crystal malt

1½ oz (45 gm) Goldings or Fuggles hops
Beer yeast
Top fermenting yeast
Water to two gallons (10 litres)

Place the dried malt extract and crystal malt into a preserving pan with a gallon (5 litres) of water. Bring to the boil and add the hops. Continue to boil for half an hour. Strain through a sterilised strainer. Mash the remaining grains with one to two pints (½–1 litre) of very hot water. Make up to two gallons (10 litres) with tap water. When the temperature has reached 65–70°F (18.5–21°C) add the yeast and ferment in the usual manner.

This beer is a clear amber colour although it retains all of the finest characteristics of a pale ale.

Full mash

Although this is a more expensive brew it is a superb example of a quality beer made from just malt, crystal and hops.

2 lb (1 kilo) crushed pale malt
½ lb (500 gm) crystal malt
1½ oz (45 gm) Goldings or Fuggles hops
Irish moss
Top fermenting yeast
Water treatment—for pale, light or bitter ales if necessary
Water to two gallons (10 litres)

Bring one gallon (5 litres) of water (treated if necessary) to 170°F (77°C). Thoroughly mix the malt and crystal malt, stir rapidly into the hot water. Adjust the temperature to 148—152°F (64—66°C) and maintain for at least two hours, or overnight if using the hot box method. Strain the liquid through a colander and muslin—which need not be sterilised at this stage—and sparge

with as much of the remaining two gallons (10 litres) of water raised to approximately 150°F (65°C) as is necessary.

As the wort is more concentrated and extra malt is used, more sparging will be required than with light ales. Any water remaining should be added to the boiling vessel. Bring the liquid to the boil and add the hops. After 1½ hours, add the Irish moss according to the instructions. It is important to add the finings at this stage as the extra malt increases the risk of hazes developing. After a further half an hour's boiling, remove from the heat and cool rapidly. Pour through a sterilised strainer into the fermentation vessel. Add tap water to make the volume up to two gallons (10 litres). When the temperature has dropped to 65—70°F (18.5–21°C) add the yeast. Ferment in the usual way.

Mash with adjuncts

This is a cheaper beer than the previous recipe. It is nevertheless a fine strong pale ale.

2 lb (1 kilo) crushed pale malt
6 oz (180 gm) flaked rice or maize
8 oz (250 gm) sugar
Irish moss
Top fermenting yeast
Water treatment for light, pale or bitter beer
Water to two gallons (10 litres)

This beer should be made by the same technique as for the full mash method. The only modification is that the sugar should be added to the liquid that is to be boiled.

Indian Pale Ale

Strong ales, made with extra hops and malt, which would keep longer and travel better, were developed when Englishmen serving overseas demanded the traditional beers of home. Large quantities were exported to India and other parts of the world—hence the name.

These beers are far more expensive than either pale or light, but if expense is not the main consideration this type of beer is perfection.

Water—If mashing, treat soft water with chalk and gypsum.

Hops—Goldings or Fuggles preferably.

Maturation—This is both the longest maturing and keeping of the Pale ales. Ideally, it should not be drunk for three months.

Liquid malt extract

2 lb (1 kilo) liquid malt extract
8 oz (250 gm) crystal malt
1½ oz (45 gm) Goldings hops
Top fermenting yeast
Water to 2 gallons (10 litres)

Place the malt extract and one gallon (5 litres) of water in a two gallon (10 litre) preserving pan and heat, stirring thoroughly until dissolved. Pour the liquid into a sterilised fermenting bucket. Meanwhile, put the crystal malt into a saucepan, together with two pints (1 litre) of water. Bring to the boil and add the hops. Let it boil gently for half an hour. Strain the liquid into a fermenting bucket containing the malt extract solution and make the volume up to 2 gallons (10 litres) with tap water. Cool, add yeast and ferment in the usual way.

Kit—no boiling method

1 kit to make 2 gallons (10 litres) of pale ale
8 oz (250 gm) dried pale malt extract
¾ oz (20 gm) Goldings
Heading liquid

Top fermenting yeast
Water to two gallons (10 litres)

Buy a kit with the maximum content of malt extract. Try to get one that recommends that you add no more than an additional 8 oz (250 gm) of sugar but *do not add any sugar*. This is a high malt beer. Replace the recommended amount of sugar with dried pale malt extract.

Place the malt from the can into the fermenting vessel taking care to wash any remaining traces from the side of the can. Add the dried malt extract and one gallon (5 litres) of hot water. Stir thoroughly to dissolve. If any of the malt fails to dissolve an extra ½ gallon (2½ litres) of water (preferably boiling) may be added. It is better not to use more hot water than is necessary as tap water may then be used to bring the liquid down to fermentation temperature. When the temperature has dropped to 65–70°F (18.5–21°C) add the yeast.

When the initial fermentation has ceased add the hops, which should remain in the liquid until bottling. Rack, and add the heading liquid according to the maker's instructions.

By mashing

An expensive mash, but this is really high quality beer, perhaps the strongest that it is possible to make without using barley wine techniques.

3 lb (1½ kilo) crushed pale malt
12 oz (360 gm) crystal malt
1½–2oz (45–60 gm) Goldings hops
Irish moss
Top fermenting yeast
Water treatment for pale, light and bitter ale if necessary
Water to 2 gallons (10 litres)

Mix the grains thoroughly and add to 10 pints (6

litres) of water raised to 170°F (77°C) in a saucepan. Stir thoroughly to ensure that any local hot spots do not destroy the enzymes. This is very important with the higher striking temperature necessary as a result of adding more grains to the liquid. Adjust the temperature to 148—152°F (64–66°C). Maintain this for at least two hours or overnight. As far more malt is involved an iodine test may be advisable. However, starch seldom remains if the temperature is kept at the exact value for two hours. If you are unsure about it, continue mashing for a further half hour.

Strain the liquid into the boiling vessel. Have a gallon (5 litres) of liquor at 150°F (65°C) ready. You may need all the remaining water as at this high grain rate it requires far more liquid to sparge the sweet wort from the grain and to dissolve out any remaining sugar. Check occasionally that the sparged liquid coming through is noticeably sweet. When it stops tasting sweet stop sparging, and add any remaining liquid directly. Over-sparging, with such a high quantity of grain, can result in any unconverted starch being dissolved out and making the beer hazy.

Bring the two gallons (10 litres) of liquid to the boil, and add the hops. After about half an hour add the Irish moss. Continue boiling for a further half hour. Cool as quickly as possible and strain through a sieve or piece of muslin in a colander. When the temperature has dropped to 65–70°(18.5–21F°C) add the yeast. Finish the beer in the usual way.

Alternative mash with adjuncts

2 lb (1 kilo) crushed pale malt
8 oz (250 gm) flaked maize
8 oz (250 gm) crystal malt
8 oz (250 gm) demerara sugar
4 oz (125 gm) of caramel and 6 oz (180 gm) of white sugar
Irish moss
1½ oz (45 gm) Goldings hops
Top fermenting yeast
Water treatment as for lager, pale or bitter beers if necessary
Water to two gallons (10 litres)

This beer is better if made with demerara sugar, but it is cheaper to use the mixture of white sugar and caramel given above. Make it in exactly the same way as the previous recipe, except that the sugar should be added directly to the boiling liquid after the sparging operation. Stir thoroughly to ensure that the sugar does not stick to the bottom of the boiler. Ferment by the general method.

Cheaper mash

2 lb (1 kilo) crushed pale malt
12 oz (360 gm) sugar
8 oz (250 gm) flaked rice
2 oz (50 gm) caramel
Irish moss
Water treatment—for light, pale or bitter beer if necessary
Top fermenting yeast

Ensure that the flaked rice is thoroughly mixed with the crushed malt and add to 1 gallon (5 litres) of water at 165°F (70°C) and mash the beer according to the method given for mashing.

Half-mash method

This gives another malt- and hop-only beer, very similar to that given by the first mash method. This can be the basis of many experimental beers in which you can adjust the ingredients. To make a cheaper beer you can add 12–16 oz (400–

500 gm) of sugar and an extra ¾ oz (20 gm) of hops and make three gallons (15 litres) instead of two (10 litres). If you are not sure whether you require water treatment or not this is a good beer to make since you can ignore the water treatment.

2 lb (1 kilo) malt extract
1 lb (500 gm) crushed pale malt
1½ oz (45 gm) Goldings or Fuggles hops
Top fermenting yeast
Water treatment as for light, pale or bitter beers (but not essential)
Water to two gallons (10 litres)

Raise one gallon (5 litres) of water in the mashing vessel to 165–170°F (73–77°C) and add the crushed malt with constant stirring. Ignore the temperature drop and add the malt extract. Stir the mixture thoroughly to ensure that the extract has dissolved. Adjust the temperature to 150–152°F (65°C). Maintain at this temperature for at least two hours or overnight. Strain into the boiler, sparge, add the hops and boil for 1½–2 hours. Cool rapidly and strain through a sterilised sieve. Make up to two gallons (10 litres) with tap water. Add yeast at 65–70°F. Finish the beer as previously described.

Bitter

Bitter is a generic term for all light and pale ales that are served on draught. You can make any of the previous recipes and serve them draught, but you may not want to drink I.P.A. in the large quantities required to justify placing a beer on draught, because of its high alcohol content.

With special draught beers it is important to ensure that they are well-conditioned and this is achieved by storing them in a cool place from the time that fermentation ceases. Ideally, the secondary fermentation stage should be conducted at a lower temperature, 55–60°F (13–16°C) to ensure that the maximum carbon dioxide is dissolved in the liquid. Unfortunately, since fermentation often ceases at this temperature, the method is liable to fail.

If you have been used to bitters served straight from the wood do not add heading liquid. Today most people seem to prefer a good creamy head and for this reason heading compound is included in the recipes.

Most of the recipes in this section are designed to make stronger beers, relying more than the other recipes on sugar, to provide extra alcohol.

Kit beer

Kit to make two gallons (10 litres) of bitter, light or pale ale
8 oz (250 gm) sugar
1 oz (30 gm) Fuggles hops
Top fermenting yeast
Water to two gallons (10 litres)

Pour the malt extract into a bucket; wash out the can with hot water and add the sugar (dissolved in warm water). Provide sufficient water to make to two gallons (10 litres). When the temperature has reached 65–70°F (18.5–21°C) ferment in the usual manner. Ensure that you skim off the yeast head, as a beer as light as this can show up every imperfection. Add the hops immediately when initial fermentation ceases. This is the easiest and cheapest of all the beer recipes given. Unfortunately, it tends to lack the quality of many of the other beers. Nevertheless it is very refreshing and surprisingly strong.

Dried malt extract method

1½ lb (750 gm) dried pale malt extract
½ lb (250 gm) sugar
½ lb (250 gm) crystal malt
1½ oz (45 gm) Fuggles hops
Top fermenting yeast
Water to two gallons (10 litres)

Place all the ingredients, except the yeast, in a preserving pan with as near to two gallons (10 litres) of water as is practical. Heat the mixture, stirring vigorously to ensure that none of the sugar sticks to the bottom of the pan. If you have had difficulties clearing previous beers add Irish moss at this stage. Otherwise omit this. When the mixture boils, partially cover the pan and maintain the boil for half an hour. Strain the liquid into the fermenting vessel and make the volume up to two gallons (10 litres). When the temperature has dropped to 65–70°F (18.5–21°C) add the yeast and ferment. This is another very easy beer to make.

Liquid malt extract

2 lb (1 kilo) liquid pale malt extract
6 oz (180 gm) sugar
6 oz (180 gm) crystal malt
2 oz (50 gm) Fuggles hops
Heading liquid
Top fermenting yeast
Water to three gallons (15 litres)

Boil the liquid malt extract, crystal malt and hops together with 1–1½ gallons (5–7 litres) of water. Slightly more aromatic beers are obtained if the hops are added after the liquid has reached the boil, but if you prefer, add the hops to the cold liquid. Ensure that the liquid is thoroughly stirred until the malt extract has completely dissolved. Boil for 30 to 45 minutes. Cool and strain.

Dissolve the sugar in the still warm liquid and add tap water to make the total volume up to three gallons (15 litres). At 65–70°F (18.5–21°C) add the yeast; add the heading liquid when the initial fermentation has ceased.

Half-mash method

2 lb (1 kilo) liquid malt extract
2 lb (1 kilo) crushed pale malt
1 lb (500 gm) sugar
Caramel to desired colour
3 oz (90 gm) Fuggles hops
Heading liquid
Top fermenting yeast
Water treatment, for pale, light or bitter beers
Water to five gallons (25 litres)

This is a cheap relatively low-gravity beer. It is low in body because of the high sugar content. Due to the lack of malt, even though it is partially mashed, it is essential to use a heading liquid. It has the advantage over the other recipes given that for the quantity of malt used an extra gallon of beer is obtained for the price of a pound of sugar.

Place the crushed malt and malt extract in the pan together with a gallon and a half of water. Heat while stirring to 148–152°F (64–66°C) to ensure that all the extract dissolves without sticking. Maintain this temperature for at least two hours or overnight in a hot box. Strain the liquid into the boiling vessel. Sparge with about one gallon (5 litres) of water at approximately 150°F (65°C). Do not worry too much about the accuracy of the temperature. Make the volume up to five gallons (25 litres) and add the sugar. If you do not possess a large enough container you may boil up three gallons only and add the remaining liquid prior to fermentation.

When the liquid has reached the boil add the

hops. Continue boiling for two hours. Strain the liquid and cool as rapidly as possible, strain into the fermenting vessel and adjust the volume with tap water to five gallons (25 litres). When the temperature has dropped to 65–70°F (18.5–21°C) add the yeast and adjust the colour by the addition of caramel dissolved in the minimum amount of water. Add the heading liquid at the cessation of primary fermentation.

Mashing

6 lb (2½ kilo) crushed pale malt
1 lb (500 gm) flaked rice or flaked maize
1 lb (500 gm) sugar
3 oz (90 gm) Fuggles hops
Irish moss
Top fermenting yeast
Water treatment for pale, light or bitter beer if necessary
Water to five gallons (25 litres)

Raise the temperature of two gallons (10 litres) of water to 165–170°F (75–77°C) in the mashing vessel. Add the malt and adjunct, stirring well to avoid any hot spots. Adjust the temperature to 150–152°F and maintain the value for at least two hours or overnight. Strain the grains through a sieve and sparge with one gallon (5 litres) at 150°F (65°C). Make up the total volume to approximately five gallons (25 litres) and bring to the boil. Add the hops and maintain the boil for two hours. About half an hour before the end of the boil add the Irish moss. Immediately the boiling has ceased shock cool the liquid. At about 70–80°F (21–25°C) strain into the fermentation bucket. Add the yeast at the usual temperature and adjust the colour by the addition of caramel. Ferment in the usual way. If you like a well-developed head on the beer, add heading liquid after the primary fermentation has ceased.

Mashed bitter

6 lb (3 kilo) crushed pale malt
10 oz (300 gm) crystal malt
12 oz (360 gm) sugar
Irish moss
Water treatment for pale, light or bitter beer if necessary
Water to five gallons (25 litres)

Make the beer by the technique given in the previous recipe, mixing the malt and crystal malt together before mashing. This is a fuller, better quality beer than the one above although more expensive to make.

Brown Ales

Brown ales probably vary more than any other type of beer. Not only do these differ in their colour but also in their taste and flavour. The most noticeable characteristic of the beer is the very pronounced maltiness with light hopping, the reverse of the pale ales where it is the hop flavour that predominates. The beers have a residual sweetness which must be provided by a non-fermentable sugar or an artificial sweetener. A good head is essential in a brown ale and you may find it necessary to incorporate heading liquid, even in recipes where it is not stipulated.

Water–When you are mashing or half-mashing, soft water is required. If you live in a soft water area, just add ½ teaspoonful of salt per gallon of water used for the mash but not for topping up. If you live in a hard water area use brown ale, water treatment.

Hops—Fuggles

Yeast—use a top-fermenting yeast

Clearing—with dark beers hazes tend to be

unnoticeable and Irish moss is generally not necessary unless you intend exhibiting. However do not be careless with your mash, as *heavy starch hazes* can be easily detected.

Colouring—In part this is provided by dark and black malts, but the majority of the colour is provided by adding caramel either at the boiling or fermenting stage. Always add caramel in small amounts until the right colour is obtained.

Maturation: These usually benefit from being kept for 2 weeks to a month after bottling.

Kit brown

One brown ale kit to make two gallons (10 litres)
4 oz (125 gm) dark malt
8 oz (250 gm) sugar
½ oz (15 gm) Fuggles hops
Top fermenting yeast
Water to two gallons (10 litres)

This beer can be made without boiling the ingredients but better results are obtained if they are boiled together for half an hour. If you do not possess a boiling pan large enough to hold the gallon of water (5 litres) in which the ingredients are to be boiled, then dissolve the malt in hot water and dry hop. If you are not satisfied with this beer try replacing a further ounce of sugar by an equal amount of crystal malt. Boil the crystal malt for twenty minutes and add the liquid obtained by straining to the malt of the kit. Should you require a sweeter beer then dissolve one or two saccharins (but no more) in hot water. Make the beer by the general method given for kit beers.

Half mash

2 lb (1 kilo) diastatic malt extract
4 oz (125 gm) black malt
4 oz (125 gm) crystal malt
1 oz (30 gm) Fuggles or Northern Brewer hops
1 or 2 saccharins
Heading liquid
Top fermenting yeast
Water to two gallons (10 litres)

This is really a superb beer well worth the extra effort involved in its production.

Heat about a gallon of water to 160°F (71°C). Add the crystal malt and black malt and then the malt extract. Stir until the malt extract is dissolved. Check the temperature and raise to 146–150°F (63–65°C) with hot water if necessary. Maintain this temperature for at least two hours or overnight. Strain, sparge with a gallon of water at 140–150°F (59–65°C). Bring to the boil and then add the hops. After two hours strain. Cool as quickly as possible. Adjust to two gallons. Add yeast at 65–70°F (18.5–21°C) and add the heading liquid after the cessation of primary fermentation.

Should you require a sweet brown, add the ground-up saccharins to the boiling liquid. If you prefer to use lactose, dissolve 2 oz (50 gm) in a small quantity of boiling water and add to the boil. If you prefer a softer beer then reduce the quantity of black malt by half, and for a sweeter beer increase the lactose.

If you do not wish to use the half-mash method then replace the 4 oz (125 gm) of black malt with dark malt and make the beer either by boiling the ingredients together (except the yeast) or simply by adding hot water.

The basic recipe given is an all-malt recipe: you can if you wish add up to half a pound (250 gm) of sugar to produce a stronger beer. Alternatively you can add an extra 12 oz (360 gm) sugar and increase the crystal malt to half pound (250 gm) to make three gallons (15 litres). When making three gallons, use 1½ oz (45 gm) hops.

Dried malt extract

1½ lb (750 gm) dried pale malt extract
8 oz (250 gm) dried dark malt extract
8 oz (250 gm) crystal malt
caramel to colour
1–2 saccharins or 2 oz (50 gm) lactose
Heading liquid
1¼ oz (35 gm) Fuggles hops
Top fermenting yeast
Water to two gallons (10 litres)

Boil the crystal malt and the two dried malt extracts together for half an hour, in one to two gallons (5–10 litres) of water depending upon the size of your pan. Add the crushed saccharin tablets (or a solution of lactose) to the boiling liquid, add the hops and strain. Allow to cool. Adjust volume to two gallons (10 litres) and add caramel to give correct colour. Add yeast and ferment in the usual way. Put in the heading liquid prior to fermentation. As with the previous recipes, up to 8 oz (250 gm) of sugar may be added for a higher alcohol beer. A cheaper beer can be made by adding 12 oz (360 gm) of sugar, 4 oz (125 gm) crystal malt, ½ oz (15 gm) hops and one extra gallon (5 litres) of water.

Mashed brown I

This recipe produces a sweet brown ale (the sweetness can of course be decreased), but if you prefer a drier beer it is better to use this alternative recipe.

7 lb (3 kilo) crushed pale malt
1 lb (500 gm) crushed dark malt or

8 oz (250 gm) crushed black malt
8 oz (250 gm) flaked maize or rice (optional)
8 oz (250 gm) lactose or 7 saccharin tablets
1 lb (500 gm) sugar
2 oz (60 gm) Fuggles or Northern Brewer hops
Caramel colour
Top fermenting yeast
Water treatment—for making dark or mild beers if necessary.
Water to five gallons (25 litres)

The maize and rice provide extra starch and hence sugar. These may be omitted but the resulting beer will be fractionally weaker and lower in body. Should you prefer a beer that is lower in alcohol, omit some—or all—of the sugar.

Thoroughly mix the malts and any adjuncts and add to the two and a half gallons (12½ litres) brewing water raised to 170°F (77°C) stirring continuously. If the temperature has dropped below 146–148°F (63°C) raise it to this value with hot water and maintain this temperature for two hours or overnight. Strain and sparge with one or two gallons (5–10 litres) of water at 140–150°F (60–65°C). Transfer to the boiler and make up to five gallons (25 litres) with tap water. Bring the liquid to the boil and add the hops. Dissolve the lactose or saccharin in the minimum amount of water and add to the beer boiling liquid. Add the caramel at this stage to adjust colour. Samples may be taken from the liquid to check the colour. After two hours shock cool and strain. Adjust the volume of liquid to five gallons (25 litres) at 67–70°F (18.5–21°C) add the yeast and ferment. When the primary fermentation has ceased you can add the heading liquid if you wish or even dry hop—although this style of beer has a low hop content.

Mashed brown II

This gives a far drier, lower-bodied brown ale.

6 lb (3 kilo) crushed pale malt
8 oz (250 gm) crushed dark malt
4 oz (125 gm) of black malt
1 oz (30 gm) crystal malt
1 lb.(500 gm) sugar
Caramel (for colour)
Top fermenting yeast
Water treatment for dark ales
Water to five gallons (25 litres)

Make the beer as in the previous method, but with crystal malt as well as the other malts. If you wish to serve these brown ales as draught, adjust the quantity of heading liquid, or leave it out completely.

Mild Ales

Mild ale shows some marked differences from brown ale. Unlike brown it is usually served with a less pronounced head and is often lower in alcohol content.

Hops—Like brown ale, this is a low-hopped drink. Use either Norther Brewer to give a strong bitter taste or Fuggles for a more mellow taste, or a mixture of both.

Water—If you live in a soft water area, add half a teaspoonful of salt per gallon (5 litres) of water for mashed beers. If you live in a hard water area, add brown or mild beer treatment.

Kit beer

Kit to make two gallons (10 litres) mild or brown ale

4 oz (125 gm) dried pale malt extract
4 oz (125 gm) dried dark malt extract
8 oz (250 gm) sugar
1 oz (25 gm) Northern Brewer or Fuggles hops
Caramel if necessary
Top fermenting yeast
Tap water to 3 gallons (15 litres)

First method

Boil the hops in two pints (1 litre) of water in a saucepan for half an hour, strain the liquid into the fermenting bucket containing the malt from the kit, the extra dried malt and the sugar. Add more hot (preferably boiling) water until all the solids are dissolved. Make up to three gallons (15 litres) with tap water.

Second method

Place the malt extract from the kit, the extra malt, sugar and hops in two gallons (10 litres) of water. Heat, stirring constantly so that none of the sugar sticks to the bottom of the pan and burns. Raise to boiling and maintain at this temperature for half an hour. Strain and make up to three gallons (15 litres).

With either method, caramel can be stirred into the total volume of liquid. To avoid difficulties it is best to take a quantity of liquid out to dissolve the caramel. Raise the temperature to ensure that all the solid has dissolved, and return to the bulk. If extra sweetness is required add lactose at the rate of one ounce per gallon (30 gm per 5 litres) or 1 saccharin tablet per gallon (5 litres). Either should be dissolved in the same manner as the caramel.

Whichever method is used to prepare the wort, it should be made up to three gallons and fermented when the temperature has dropped to 65–70°F (18.5–21°C).

4 lb (2 kilo) dried pale malt extract
1 lb (500 gm) dried dark malt extract
1 lb (500 gm) demerara sugar
1½ lb (750 gm) Fuggles or Northern Brewer
hops
Caramel to colour
Top fermenting yeast
Water to five gallons (25 litres)

Place all the ingredients, except the yeast and caramel, in two and a half gallons (12½ litres) of water. Stir thoroughly to ensure that the sugar does not burn. Bring to the boil and maintain for half an hour. Strain into a fermenting bucket. This is the better method, but if you do not possess a large enough utensil, boil the hops for half an hour in two pints (1 litre) of water. Strain the liquid into the fermenting bucket containing the solids dissolved in four gallons (20 litres) of very hot water. Add the caramel to colour and if you require a sweeter beer, five ounces (150 gm) of lactose or 5 saccharin tablets. Allow the temperature to drop to 65–70°F (18.5–21°C) and ferment in the usual way.

White sugar may be substituted for demerara as an economy measure.

Half mash method

to make five gallons (25 litres)

1 lb (½ kilo) pale malt
2 lb (1 kilo) pale malt extract
1 lb (½ kilo) crushed dark malt
Lactose or saccharin optional
1 lb (500 gm) demerara sugar
2 oz (60 gm) Fuggles or Northern Brewer hops
Water treatment for dark ale
Caramel to colour
Top fermenting yeast
Water to five gallon (25 litres)

Raise one and a half gallons (7 litres) of treated water to 170°F (77°C) and pour the grain malts into the water. Add the malt extract and raise the temperature to 146–148°F (63–64°C) by the addition of hot water. Maintain this temperature for two hours or overnight. Strain the liquid into the boiling vessel and sparge with about a gallon (5 litres) of water raised to 140–150°F (60–65°C). Add the sugar to the warm water and stir until dissolved. Add the lactose or saccharin if desired, and make the total volume up to five gallons (25 litres). Bring to the boil and add the hops. Maintain the boil for about two hours, adding the necessary caramel. Shock cool, strain, make up to five gallons (25 litres) with tap water and ferment.

Mashed mild ale

2 lb (1 kilo) crushed malt
8 oz (250 gm) dark malt
1 lb (500 gm) crystal malt
8 oz (250 gm) white sugar
1 lb (500 gm) demerara sugar
Caramel
5 oz (150 gm) lactose or 5 saccharin tablets
(optional)
2½ oz (65 gm) Fuggles hops
Top fermenting yeast
Water treatment for dark beers
Water to five gallons (25 litres)

Place all the well-mixed grains in 1 gallon (5 litres) of water, (do not use a larger volume), raised to 170°F (77°C). After stirring thoroughly adjust the temperature with hot water to 146–148°F (60–64°C). Maintain this temperature for eight hours or overnight. Strain and sparge with a gallon (5 litres) of water raised to 140–150°F (60–65°C). Dissolve the sugar in the hot liquid and increase the volume to five gallons (25 litres). Bring to the boil, add the hops and the lactose or saccharin dissolved in either hot water or a small quantity of the wort. Caramel should be added at this stage to give the pale colour. After two hours strain the wort into the fermenting vessel and make up to five gallons (25 litres) at 65–70°F (18.5–21°C). Add the yeast and ferment in the usual way.

Dry or Irish Stout

Dry stout is the fullest of all beers. The extra body is balanced by bitterness and characterised by the well-developed head that should remain in the glass until the final mouthful is drunk. Good dry stouts can only be produced by using both a high pale malt rate and a high hop rate with roast barley to give depth of taste. Keep the recipe simple by adding no extra sugar and adjust the bitterness through the hopping rate.

It is usually necessary to add heading liquid to all recipes. I have found that both the taste and head retention characteristics of home brewed stouts are fine, but the head often tends to have a brown tinge to it rather than the ideal creamy white colour. This does not detract from the taste but gives me an excuse to continue experimenting with what I consider to be the finest of all beers.

Dry stouts can either be bottled or on draught, but with draught beers you may find it necessary to increase the quantity of heading liquid.

Only three methods are given for making Irish stout as it is difficult to make a good quality beer from dried malt extract. Also dry stout is universally known and there is little demand for variations.

Hops—Northern Brewer

Yeast—Top fermenting beer yeast

Water—This beer can be made with most waters. However soft water can be improved by the addition of half a teaspoon of chalk per gallon. Hard water straight from the tap is ideal for mashing, unless it contains a great deal of temporary hardness in which case it should be boiled for half an hour.

Maturation—It can be drunk after a month after bottling but it is at its best after 3–6 months.

From kits

Providing both dried malt and hops are added, very good dry stouts can be made from kit beers.

1 kit to make 2 gallons (10 litres) of Irish stout
4 oz (125 gm) dark dried malt extract
½ oz (15 gm) Northern Brewer hops
Sugar as given in the instructions
Heading liquid
Water to fourteen pints or two gallons (9–10 litres)

Place the contents of the kit in the fermentation bucket with the sugar and extra malt. Boil the hops, initially half an ounce (15 gm) in 2 pint (¾ litre) of water, although you may wish to use up to twice this amount in later brews. Strain, and add the liquid to the fermenting bucket. Do not dry hop Irish stouts, it is the bitter characteristic extracted by boiling, rather than the aromatic flavourings obtained by dry hopping, that we are trying to achieve. Make the total volume up to two gallons (10 litres) with hot water. If you find that the beer still lacks body, add water to bring the total up to fourteen pints (9 litres). By adjusting hopping rates, and the amount of water added, it is possible to make a dry stout that will satisfy the most discerning palate. Ferment at 65–70°F (18.5–21°C) and add the heading liquid after primary fermentation has taken place.

You can boil the extract, dried malt and sugar with the hops for half an hour as an alternative, but I have found no advantage in using this variation. Caramel should not be necessary when making this beer from kits.

Half-mash

I prefer this method when making dry stouts. It takes longer than using kits and requires a large vessel for mashing, but is well worth the extra effort.

To make three gallons (15 litres)

2 lb (1 kilo) diastatic malt extract
2½ oz (2.2 kilo) crushed pale malt
½ lb (250 gm) roast barley (use black or dark malt if not available)
2½ oz (75 gm) Northern Brewer hops
Water treatment as recommended
Heading liquid
Top fermenting yeast
Water to three gallons (15 litres)

Raise one and a half gallons (7.5 litres) of brewing water to 160°F (71°C) and stir in the thoroughly-mixed grains. Then add the malt extract. The temperature will have dropped below the required 148–152°F (64–66°C), so raise to this level with hot water and maintain for two hours or overnight. At such a high malting rate, inefficient mashing is more likely than with other beers, but hazes can seldom be detected in such a dark full-bodied beer. Testing for starch with iodine may be omitted, although of course if you wish to examine the efficiency of mashing, you can test and increase the time period if necessary.

Sparge with one gallon (5 litres) of water raised to 140–150°F (60–65°C). Bring the liquid to the boil, add the hops, and continue heating for two hours. Shock cool, strain and make up to three gallons (15 litres). Add the yeast at 65–70°F (18.5–21°C) and the heading liquid when the primary fermentation is complete.

Full mash

A lot of work but a superb beer.

8 lb (3½ kilo) crushed pale malt
1 lb (500 gm) crushed roast barley (or black or dark malt)
4 oz (125 gm) Northern Brewer
Top fermenting yeast
Water treatment as recommended
Water to five gallons (25 litres)

This is a far simpler recipe than the other mashes discussed and there is no real difference in the mashing technique even though much more grain is used. Do not be tempted to over-sparge, nor to use more than the recommended amount of sparging water. Not only will this result in too much liquid to be boiled off, but any unconverted starch may be dissolved out of the spent grains also.

Bring three and a half gallons (17½ litres) of water to 170°F (77°C) and add the grains stirring constantly. Adjust the temperature to 148–150°F (64–65°C) and maintain this level for two hours or overnight. Strain and sparge with two gallons (10 litres) of water into the boiler, (the excess water will be evaporated off during boiling). Bring to the boil, add the hops and maintain the boiling for two hours. If you experience any major clearing difficulties increase this period by half an hour. Shock cool, strain and adjust to five gallons (25 litres) with tap water. At 65–70°F add the yeast. Even with this full mash I find it necessary to add about half the normal amount of heading liquid after the primary fermentation is complete.

Sweet Stout

This drink is also known as milk stout. The origin of this name has been attributed to the use of lactose, which is a sugar obtained from milk. Another possibility is that it is derived from the drinking habits of nursing mothers, taking stout with an equal volume of milk.

It is similar to certain types of brown ale, but fuller and sweeter.

Water—as for brown ales, soft water is best. If you have soft water, simply add half a teaspoon of salt. If you have hard water treat as for brown ale.

Hops—Use Fuggles if you do not wish to have a pronounced bitter taste. If you prefer a bitter taste use Northern Brewer.

Sweetening—Use either lactose at the rate of 1–2 oz per gallon (5–12 gm per litre) or saccharin at the rate of one tablet per gallon (5 litres).

Yeast—Top fermenting yeast.

From kits

It is unlikjely that you would want to sweeten a kit beer and you will probably not need to increase the hopping rate. To improve the quality simply make seven pints (4½ litres) for every gallon (5 litres) recommended or add two to four ounces (50–125 gm) of dried malt per gallon (5 litres) of beer. You are almost certain to want to improve the head retaining characteristics.

1 kit to make two gallons (10 litres) of sweet stout
4–8 oz (125–250 gm) dried malt extract
8 oz (250 gm) sugar
Head retaining liquid
Top fermenting yeast
Water to two gallons (10 litres)

Place the kit, malt extract, sugar and dried malt in a preserving pan, together with a gallon (5 litres) of water, and warm until dissolved then bring to the boil. After boiling for about ten minutes transfer to the fermenting bucket. If you do not possess a large pan, place the ingredients in the bucket, add a gallon of boiling water and stir until dissolved.

Make up to two gallons (10 litres) with tap water. At 65–70°F (18.5–21°C) add the yeast. The head retaining liquid should be added after primary fermentation has ceased. Should you feel that extra hopping is necessary, boil ½–1 oz (15–30 gm) Fuggles hops for a subsequent brew. This liquid should be added to the malt prior to placing in the fermenting vessel.

From dried malt extract

1¾ lb (850 gm) dried pale malt extract
4 oz (125 gm) dried dark malt extract
8 oz (250 gm) sugar
3 oz (90 gm) lactose (or two saccharin tablets)
1 oz (30 gm) Northern Brewer hops or 1½ oz (40 gm) Fuggles hops
Caramel
Head retention liquid
Top fermenting yeast
Water to two gallons (10 litres)

Place dried malt extract, and both sugars (household and lactose) in a preserving pan or saucepan with a gallon (5 litres) of water and bring to the boil, ensuring that none of the material sticks to the bottom of the pan. When the liquid is boiling, add the hops and maintain the boil for twenty minutes to half an hour. Strain into the fermenting bucket, and make up to two gallons (10 litres). If necessary dissolve some caramel in the minimum amount of water and add to the liquid. Add yeast, ferment and provide the head retaining liquid in the usual manner.

From liquid malt extract

2 lb (1 kilo) diastatic malt extract
8 oz (250 gm) dried pale malt extract
12 oz (360 gm) sugar
5 oz (125 gm) lactose (or saccharin)
1½ oz (45 gm) Northern Brewer hops or 2 oz (60 gm) Fuggles
Caramel
Head retention liquid
Yeast
Water to three gallons (15 litres)

Make the beer in the same manner as from dried malt extract, placing the liquid extract together with the dried malt in the preserving pan.

Half mash method

2 lb (1 kilo) diastatic malt extract
1 lb (500 gm) crushed pale malt
1 lb (500 gm) crushed dark malt
or 12 oz (360 gm) black malt
6–8 oz (200 gm) lactose or 5 saccharin tablets
3 oz (90 gm) Northern Brewer hops
or 4 oz (125 gm) Fuggles
Caramel
Top fermenting yeast
Water to five gallons (25 litres)

Raise two gallons (10 litres) of water to 170°F (77°C) then add the thoroughly mixed grains and malt extract stirring constantly. Adjust the temperature to 148–150°F (64–65°C) and maintain for at least two hours or overnight in a hot box. Strain and sparge with two gallons (10 litres) water into the boiling vessel, add the sugar and lactose (or saccharin). Make up to approximately five gallons (25 litres) with tap water and boil. Add the hops at the boiling stage. Remove some of the wort, examine its colour and add the necessary caramel dissolved in the hot wort. Continue boiling for two hours. Shock cool, strain and make up to five gallons (25 litres). Add the yeast at 65–70°F (18.5–21°C). With a correctly conducted mash there should be no need to add heading liquid, but if you are not satisfied, add it to the next batch.

Full mash

3 lb (1.5 kilo) crushed pale malt
8 oz (250 gm) crushed dark malt or
4 oz (125 gm) black malt
8 oz (250 gm) flaked maize
2½ oz (75 gm) Northern Brewer Hops or 3 oz (90 gm) Fuggles hops
Caramel
6–8 oz (200 gm) or 4 saccharin tablets
Top fermenting yeast
Water to five gallons (25 litres)

This gives a cheaper, lighter-bodied stout which possesses less body and therefore cannot take quite as much sweetening or hops.

Mix all the grains thoroughly and then make the beer by the method given in the previous recipe for half-mashed stout.

Lager

This most popular of drinks often proves to be a disappointment to home brewers. It need not be but it is important to pay very close attention to detail when brewing, especially to ensure that no gum remains in contact with liquid during the fermentation.

As with light ales the beer has so delicate a flavour and such a low body, any imperfection is readily detectable. Using a bottom fermenting yeast, there are very few yeast cells at the top of the liquid and all the frothy head may safely be removed. For the best results always use a lager yeast which will be tolerant of far lower temperatures than top-acting yeasts. Lager yeast will generally ferment out in the garage even during winter once the initial fermentation is complete. Where low temperature fermentations are being conducted, it is essential to check that fermentation has not stopped. If you think that the beer has ceased working prematurely, bring it into a warm atmosphere and if necessary add a fresh sample of yeast.

Later fermentation can take up to two months to complete and the maturation period should be at least six months.

If the beer is left in the presence of a large volume of air for this period of time infection resulting in vinegaring of the beer is likely to occur. To avoid this, always transfer the beer to a demijohn when conducting a prolonged fermentation after the primary fermentation. Fill to within an inch and fit an air lock.

Conditioning is important with all beers, but to obtain the flavour of lager special care should be taken to ensure that the fermentation in the bottle or barrel is conducted at the same low temperature as the other stages. This, again, is time-consuming so do not bother to go to this trouble while you are building up your stocks. When you have established your stocks, then brew your lagers six months before they are required.

Many commercial lagers are made from special malts, produced from different varieties of barley than those used for pale ales. The sugars are extracted by decoction mashing, which involves mashing different ingredients at different temperatures and blending the worts. These practices, which may appear to be beyond the amateur, are not essential. Whilst I would always recommend you to use a true lager malt if you can obtain it, it is possible to make a drink very similar to lager from standard pale malt and even from top fermenting yeasts. If you cannot obtain the correct ingredients and do not wish to conduct a low temperature fermentation do not be detered, but be prepared to accept a slightly lower standard of beer. Never use crystal malt in lager production.

Hops—One of the secrets of lager-making is the hopping. Go to the trouble of obtaining either Saaz or Hallertau hops. It is the aromaticity rather than the bitterness that is most pronounced in a good lager. It is not worth making this type of beer unless you do have the correct hop variety and dry hopping is virtually essential, use about one third of the hops given in the recipe in this way.

Water—Lager requires a soft water. Should you have hard water soften it by boiling for half an hour and decanting from the precipitate formed. Where methods other than mashing are used tap water is adequate.

If you experience difficulties with fermentation add half a teaspoon of lactic or citric acid per gallon (5 litres) prior to adding the yeast.

From kits

1 kit to make two gallons (10 litres) of lager
4 oz (125 gm) dried pale malt extract
8 oz (250 gm) sugar
½ oz (15 gm) of Saaz or Hallertau hops
Heading liquid
Water to fourteen pints or two gallons (9–10 litres)

Make the lager according to the instructions on the label, except when you add the sugar also add the extra malt. Take special care to skim off the gum and yeast from the top of the fermenting liquid. Add all the extra hops at the dry hopping stage. This hopping rate can be adjusted with experience. Ferment in a demijohn as described for lagers. Add the heading liquid with thorough stirring prior to placing in bottles or the barrel.

Should you find the lager too thin (but remember lager is a very light bodied beer) use all the ingredients given, but make only fourteen pints (9 litres) of beer.

Read also the general instructions on lager-making.

From malt extract

2 lb (1 kilo) diastatic malt extract
4 oz (125 gm) sugar
1½–2 oz (45–60 gm) Saaz or Hallertau hops
Heading liquid
Bottom fermenting yeast
Water to two gallons (10 litres)

It may seem that the recipe could take more sugar, but over-sugaring is a common fault found more often with this type of beer than any other.

To make the beer, boil the malt with a gallon (5 litres) of water and add two thirds of the hops when the liquid has reached the boil. Maintain the boil for twenty minutes. Strain into the fermenting vessel, and make up to two gallons (10 litres). Conduct the fermentation, dry hopping, and the addition of the heading liquid, as described in the introduction to the lager-making recipes. If you experience any difficulties with the clearing of the beer and finings have no effect, add Irish moss with the hops in your next brew.

Mashing

In spite of the complexity of commercial practices I find that very fair lagers can be produced by mashing for two hours at 150°F (65°C) and would recommend this method to the general kitchen brewer. If you possess a heater with an accurate thermostat try a mash heated to 130°F (54°C) for half an hour and then raised to 150°F (65°C) for the remaining one and a half hours. I think you will agree that compared with other variables such as hopping rate, the difference in character of the beer is negligible. If you experience any clearing problems try adding Irish moss half an hour before the end of the boil (this should not be necessary).

Half mash

2 lb (1 kilo) diastatic malt extract
2 lb (1 kilo) lager malt or pale malt if not obtainable
1 lb (500 gm) sugar
3½ oz (100 gm) Saaz or Hallertau hops
Heading liquid
Top fermenting lager yeast
Water treatment: soften the water if necessary
Water to five gallons (25 litres)

Raise ten pints (6 litres) of water to 160°F (71°C), add the crushed pale malt and the diastatic malt stirring constantly, and raise the temperature back to 160°F (71°C).
Maintain this temperature for two hours. If clarity proves to be a problem when carrying out the starch test continue heating until the starch has disappeared. (Generally, though, this stage may be omitted.) Strain and sparge into the boiler with one gallon (5 litres) of water, and make the total volume up to five gallons (25 litres). Bring to the boil and add two-thirds of the hops, retain

the remainder for dry hopping. Boil for two hours. Shock cool, strain into the fermenting bucket and make the volume up to 5 gallons (25 litres). Ferment and finish as described in the introduction to lager-making.

Full mash without adjuncts

5 lb (2.5 kilo) crushed lager or pale malt
Up to 1 lb (500 gm) sugar (optional)
3½ oz (100 gm) Saaz or Hallertau hops
Heading liquid
Bottom fermenting yeast
Water to two gallons (10 litres)

You may use any quantity up to a pound of household sugar—do not be tempted to use other types with this recipe. I would suggest that you start with half a pound. Add the crushed malt to two gallons (10 litres) of water and make the beer as described for the half-mash.

Full mash with adjuncts

Generally I feel that adjuncts are more of an economy measure than a means of improving the quality of the beer. However, they do tend to have a more noticeable effect on the delicate flavour of lager, and you may like to try this brew which includes flaked maize.

4 lb (2 kilo) crushed lager or pale malt
8 oz (250 gm) flaked maize
8 oz (250 gm) sugar
3½ oz (100 gm) Saaz or Hallertau hops
Heading liquid
Bottom fermenting yeast
Water to five gallons (25 litres)

Mix together the crushed malt and maize, add to two gallons (10 litres) of water at 160°F (71°C) and conduct the brewing as described under the mash method.

If you like this beer another variation increases the flaked maize to one pound (500 gm) with or without the sugar. If you can obtain malted wheat, this can be used in place of the flaked maize.

Alternatively, you may use these adjuncts instead of one pound of crushed pale malt or in addition to the other ingredients in the half-mash method.

Barley Wine

Like lager, barley wine is so different from all other beers that special methods are necessary for its preparation. Ideally barley wine should have an alcohol strength of 8–10%, somewhere between two and three times the strength of most other beers. It is similar to pale ales, being light in colour with a pronounced hop flavour, but it has a mature taste. Barley wines are the king of beers—expensive to make and requiring patience—but once tasted you know that it is all worthwhile.

A good barley wine will keep for several years, just how long I cannot say, since all mine have been drunk way before any sign of deterioration was noted . . .

Being so high in alcohol, they require a starting gravity in the region of 1.070—1.080. Extracting liquids of this density by mashing is fraught with danger, unless you have the proper equipment and are prepared to experiment and accept a few disappointments. I make all my barley wine from diastatic malt extract or kits, and would strongly advise you to do the same. However, I have included a half-mash and a full mash which work, for the enthusiast. If you are mashing, then the water should be the same as employed for light and pale ales.

Whichever method you use to make the wort the fermentation technique is the same.

Barley Wines—since barley wines have the same concentration as light table wines, wine-making fermentation techniques must be used. Therefore the best results are obtained from wine yeast (and pouring the drink very carefully), or by using 'Beerbrite' caps which will overcome the yeast sediment problem.

When the wort in the fermentation bucket has reached a temperature of 65—70°F (18.5–21°C), a temperature which should be maintained throughout the fermentation, add a teaspoon of yeast. Remove any gummy deposits as they form but retain slightly more of the creamy head. After the initial voluminous head has subsided, rack the beer off, into a demijohn, and fit an airlock. After a month, or when half an inch (1 cm) of sediment has formed at the bottom of the jar, rack the beer into a clean sterilised container and again fit an airlock. Rack again when a similar quantity of lees has reformed. After a month the beer should be clear, providing the temperature has been maintained; if it has not the process will take longer. It should be racked once again into a sterilised bucket or other container prior to bottling. The racking is important for two reasons. The lees will begin to decompose if left and give the beer a musty taste. Small quantities of air dissolve in the beer when it is being racked and this helps the yeast to continue fermenting in the presence of moderately high alcohol concentrations.

All air should be excluded from the liquid after the primary fermentation has ceased. However, the very small quantities obtained during racking, while insufficient to support the acetic acid-forming yeast, are just enough to aid alcohol-producing yeasts. Great care should be taken to ensure that the racking tube is sterilised on every occasion before use to prevent contamination by other spoilage yeasts.

It is advisable to bottle barley wine in half pint bottles due to its strength. Prime the bottles with sugar at the rate of a quarter of a level 5 ml teaspoonful to half a pint (250 ml). Take great care with this measurement as it is difficult to measure such a small amount. Any error here will result in an over- or under-primed beer.

Hops and Hopping rate—Since a large quantity of malt is employed and the beer is far more expensive than others it is well worth using the best hops, which for this particular brew is Goldings. Such a full beer requires a high hopping rate and you may use up to one ounce (30 gm) per gallon (5 litres) although initially it is better to use three quarters of this amount. About a quarter of an ounce (7 gm) of this should be used for dry hopping to produce the desired aromaticity.

These hops should be added to the fermenting bucket about a week before transferring to demijohns. If you wish to transfer to a demijohn as soon as primary fermentation has ceased— and this is the ideal time as it removes the possibility of acetic acid-forming bacteria attacking the beer—then hop oil may be added, drop by drop, to taste.

Heading liquid—If used, this should be added to the bulk of the beer prior to bottling, according to the manufacturer's instructions.

When making barley wine check the gravity with the hydrometer to ensure that there is sufficient malt present, and add dried pale malt extract to increase the gravity to 1.070—1.080.

From kits

A very satisfactory method.

One kit designed to make one gallon (5 litres)

barley wine
Sugar as given in instructions
¼ oz (7–8 gm) Goldings hops
Heading liquid
Top-fermenting yeast
Water to one gallon (5 litres)

Place the sugar and malt extract from the kit in one gallon (5 litres) of water, and bring to the boil stirring continuously. Add all the hops and continue boiling for half an hour. Strain into the fermenting bucket and add any water necessary to return the volume to one gallon (5 litres). At between 60–70°F (15–21°C) measure the gravity and make any temperature correction. One ounce (30 gm) of dried malt extract will raise the gravity of a gallon (5 litres) of wort by 0.002 so the weight to be added may be calculated. If you find that the gravity is 1.058 and you require a gravity of 1.070 then you will need to add:

$$\frac{1.070-1.058}{0.002} = 6 \text{ ounces}$$

or in metric terms 30 gm of dried malt extract raises the gravity of 5 litres of wort by approximately 0.002. So for the same beer the calculation becomes:

$$\frac{1.070-1.058}{0.002} \times 30 = 180 \text{ gm}$$

The approximations adopted make these calculations easier and will not affect the quality of the beer.

Add the calculated amount of dried malt to the minimum quantity of hot water—the slight addition of water will be more than compensated by losses as a result of skimming and racking. Do not add the solid straight to the liquid because it is unlikely to dissolve and will leave lumps of jelly-like malt in the beer.

Add the yeast and ferment the beer by the method given in the introduction.

Diastatic malt extract

2 lb (1 kilo) diastatic malt extract
8 oz (250 gm) crystal malt
1 lb (500 gm) dried malt extract
1 lb (500 gm) white sugar
1½ oz (45 gm) Goldings hops
Heading liquid
Top fermenting yeast
Water to two gallons (10 litres)

With the higher malting and hopping rate you can use far more sugar than with the lighter beer, and full advantage should be taken of this. This is one beer where you can replace white sugar with demerara and notice the effect. Place all the malts and sugars in two gallons (10 litres) of water in a boiling vessel and bring to the boil. Add one ounce (30 gm) hops, retaining the remainder for dry hopping. Boil for half an hour. Strain into a fermenting vessel, make up to two gallons (10 litres). When the temperature has dropped to 65–70°F (18.5–21°C) add the yeast and ferment as described in the introduction.

This may be used as a basic recipe from which to make barley wine. If it is not malty enough you may replace amounts of sugar with dried pale malt. Should you experience difficulties with clearing the beer add Irish moss with the hops.

Mashing

This is a very wasteful method of making this type of beer because in order to achieve the high starting gravity a far larger amount of grain than is normally encountered in brewing is used and it is also necessary to keep the volume of liquid to a minimum. Consequently sparging has to be stopped whilst sweet wort, relatively high in sugars, is still being produced.

With this beer, you may replace some or all of the sugar with demerara sugar as in the previous recipe.

Half mash

4 lb (2 kilo) diastatic malt extract
3 lb (1.5 kilo) crushed pale malt
2 lb (1 kilo) crystal malt
2 lb (1 kilo) sugar
4 oz (120 gm) Goldings hops
Irish moss
Top fermenting beer yeast
Water treatment for pale ales
Water to five gallons (25 litres)

Raise three gallons (15 litres) of water to 170°F (77°C). Add the thoroughly-mixed crushed pale malt and crystal malt stirring constantly. Quickly add the liquid extract so that the grains are at the elevated temperature for the shortest period of time. Adjust the temperature to 150–152°F (68°C) and maintain for two hours, or overnight. Strain into the boiling vessel. Sparge with two gallons (10 litres)—do not worry about the total volume exceeding five gallons (25 litres) as a fairly large amount will be lost by evaporation during the boil. It is essential to avoid waste, so sparge more slowly and with a far more even distribution of liquid than with any other type of beer.

When the sparging is complete bring the liquid to the boil and add 3 oz (90 gm) of hops, retaining the remainder for dry hopping. After boiling for two hours add the Irish moss and boil for a further half an hour—note the extra boiling period. Shock cool. Strain into the fermenting bucket, adjust to five gallons (25 litres) and when the temperature is between 65—70°F (18.5–21°C) add the yeast. Ferment by the method given in the introduction.

Full mash

8 lb (4 kilo) crushed pale malt
1 lb (500 gm) flaked maize or flaked rice
1 lb (500 gm) white sugar
1 lb (500 gm) crystal malt
4 oz (125 gm) Goldings hops
Top fermenting yeast
Water treatment for pale ale
Water to five gallons (25 litres)

Thoroughly mix the crushed pale malt, the flaked maize or rice and the crystal malt. Add with constant stirring to three and a half gallons (17½ litres) of water raised to 170°F (75°C). Proceed according to the method given under half mash.

Other Beers

XXXX is a very strong ale similar to mild, but with more body and depth. It is now less popular than it was in former years when it was sold under a variety of different names, such as Christmas ales. The easiest way to make this beer is to add either an extra half a pound per gallon (250 gm per 5 litres) of crushed malt or dried malt extract, depending upon which method you are using, to one of the standard mild recipes. This will give you an increase of 0.015 in the specific gravity with a resultant increase of about 2% in the alcohol concentration. With XXXX it is advisable to use Northern Brewer or failing this Bullion hops in the same quantity as recommended for mild. If you can only obtain Fuggles hops increase the quantity by 25%.

Sweetness and colour should be the same as for mild. Strong beers take longer to mature and keep better than weak beers.

Oatmeal Stout

This was once quite popular as a medicinal drink but since all beers might be considered in this context, I feel that there are many more pleasant ones to choose from. As oatmeal is an adjunct it requires mashing. Replace a half pound (250 gm) of crushed pale malt with half a pound (250 gm) of porridge oats in the sweet stout recipe. If you prefer a dry oatmeal stout omit the lactose or saccharin from the recipe.

Liquorice Beer

There seems to be a deep-rooted belief that liquorice is good for you, this has been taken to the extreme of adding liquorice to beers to flavour it. If you wish to make this type of ale, use either a brown or sweet stout recipe as the beer for the brew and add one ounce (30 gm) of crushed root liquorice with the hops. Such beers can be made by any method.

The only virtue I can see in making these so-called medicinal beers is that if you believe they do you good, it gives an excuse, should you need one, to drink beer!

Diabetic Beers

No one suffering from diabetes should drink any form of beer without first seeking medical approval.

If you are allowed to drink beers, then there is no reason why you should not brew your own. What you must ensure is that there is no residual sugar in the finished beer. The beers best-suited to the diabetic are the liquid malt extract kit beers that ferment down to a specific gravity of 1.000. Make according to the manufacturer's instructions, including the addition of any recommended sugar, but check the gravity with a hydrometer before drinking, until you are familiar with beer-making and the effect of the liquid on your metabolism.

An alcoholic drink can result in an increase in weight, so it is best not to boost the alcohol in the beer even though it will not result in residual sugar. To change the style adjust the hopping rate and variety. It is surprising the effect this can have on light ales and lagers (generally the most suitable to make if you suffer from diabetes).

As far as home brewed beers are concerned avoid mashed beers, with their high residual dextrins, and also beer containing adjuncts.

Chapter 9
Bottled and Draught Beer

When making either of these kinds of beer, always check that they have finished fermenting, either with an hydrometer or by tasting, and if there is the slightest doubt the beer should be left in the fermenting vessel for a few more days. It can then either be bottled or put in a container for serving draught. Some beer-makers worry about the beer being left in the fermenting vessel for too long, but if you have maintained sterile conditions throughout it will do the beer no harm. Whilst it is not good practice, beers will stay sound in a correctly sealed vessel for weeks, if not months.

Unless you intend drinking very large quantities of home-made beer, or prefer the style of draught beers, then it is better to bottle. This is particularly true while you are making small experimental batches.

The most convenient of all bottles are the old-fashioned screw top type, fitted with a rubber washer. Although these are becoming difficult to obtain they are well worth the effort of finding. Do not be deterred from buying this type of bottle if the washers have perished; it is possible to buy new washers through your home brew supplier.

If you cannot obtain screw-topped bottles then you will have to use crown capped bottles, and buy a crown capping machine and caps. Under no circumstances bottle beer in non-returnable beer bottles or lemonade bottles of any type. These are designed for drinks that are all artificially carbonated and the manufacturers can control the pressure of the carbon dioxide to within critical limits. Consequently a thinner, and cheaper bottle can be used. However carefully home-made beers are primed, there will be occasions when the pressure inside the bottle will be greater than it should be.

This increased pressure could well cause the bottles to explode. For the same reason always check bottles before using and ruthlessly discard any that are cracked or chipped.

Sterilise the bottles prior to using either with bleach (see section on kit beer-making), or with one of the proprietary sterilising agents.

Prior to bottling it is possible to make one final adjustment. If the beer does not possess a sufficiently hoppy flavour then extra hops may be provided by dry hopping. You should not need to add more than a quarter of an ounce per gallon (7 gm per 5 litres). If you do need to add more, then your initial hopping rate must have been wrong, or the hops that you used of poor quality. Should you dry hop at this stage, as a curative measure rather than as part of the planned brewing technique, you will still need to keep the beer in the fermenting bucket for about a week—an extra day or two will do no harm. Some brewers who make large quantities of beer and have more than one type at approximately the same stage of completion will blend their beers at this stage. This really only applies to exhibition beers.

With the bottles ready, syphon or strain the beer into a second sterilised container. It is easier to clear the bulk of the liquid first rather than attempt to syphon the liquid into individual bottles. Place a small sterilised funnel in the top of the bottle and place half a level 5 ml teaspoon of sugar in the funnel. Pour the beer through the funnel until it is within half an inch (1.5 cm) of the top of the bottle. The weights and volumes given in the recipes are not critical because the balance of the beer can tolerate quite wide variations. However, every effort should be made to ensure that the small quantity of sugar for priming is measured out as accurately as possible. The slightest variation can result in an under- or over-gassed beer. Styles of beer-drinking differ quite markedly from country to country: in the United States, for example, far gassier beers are enjoyed than in Britain. If you prefer a gassy beer then you can go up to twice the amount of recommended sugar for priming, but I should try it with a few bottles at first and then only bottles which normally contain very gassy beers. Whether it is a success will depend on your palate and whether the bottles that are available locally can withstand the strain. Two words of caution when opening an over-gassed bottle of beer: store it in the refrigerator first, this will decrease the pressure, and cover the bottle with a cloth when opening. With any over-gassed beer there is always the danger that you will have a liquid that comes out of the bottle in an uncontrollable manner and that the yeast sediment will be disturbed.

Another way to prime the beer is to dissolve 2–2½ oz (50–60 gm) of sugar per gallon (5 litres) in the minimum amount of water and add this to the bulk of the beer. This is certainly the best method with draught beers, but with bottled beers you must ensure that the sugar is thoroughly stirred into the liquid to distribute it evenly. The mixing of two liquids of different densities can take quite a time to occur naturally and any uneven distribution will result in some under- and some over-gassed bottles of beer. For this reason I prefer to add dry sugar to the bottles individually.

One ingredient that can be added to the beer at this stage is heading liquid. Heading liquid may be added at any stage but generally the conditioning stage is the most convenient time to add it. If you have used a combined head retention and yeast nutrient it is seldom necessary (except possibly with barley wines, when it should be added with the yeast).

The next operation is to fit the bottle with a crown cork. There are two different types of cappers on the market. The simplest and cheapest involves a cap fitted to a handle. The cork is placed inside the cap which is then placed on top of the bottle and hit with the hammer until the cap is in position. You will soon get the knack of using this device but until you do you may find it noisy and frustrating. To simplify the operation you can get a lever operated corker which basically works in the same way. It costs about four times as much as the simpler device, but with many bottles to stop it is well worth the expense.

Once the beer is inside the bottle secondary fermentation recommences. If it is left for five to ten days at 70°F (21°C) it will be ready for drinking, but will taste far better if kept longer. During this stage three vital processes take place. The first is the conversion of the priming sugar to carbon dioxide which gasses the beer.

The second process is the development of the head retention characteristics as a result of the dissolved gasses and the compounds that lower the surface tension of the liquid. The beer must not only develop a good head but it must retain it through most of its life in the glass. For a good head there must be sufficient carbon dioxide, and the liquid must possess a surface tension low enough to maintain the frothy nature of the drink. Certain compounds have the ability to lower the surface tension of a liquid and the best known example is soap suds—although I would not use them in your beer! Fortunately, compounds with the necessary head retention characteristics develop naturally within the beer, and it is only where these are insufficient that it is necessary to add heading compounds.

The ability to develop a good head depends upon several variables and generally there are far less head retention problems with mashed beers than with brews made from extracts. Today it is possible to buy artificial heading liquids such as ethylene glycol alginate, a well known food additive which can be added to the beer to overcome any deficiency in natural heading material. Some kit manufacturers are already adding this to their extracts, so never add extra heading liquid to the first batch of any type of beer that you make. Also check the list of ingredients on the can to make sure it has not been added already. Head development, the depth of the froth and head retention are themselves dependent upon different factors, but you will find that once a good head develops it almost invariably remains for an acceptable period of time in the glass. Artificial heading materials are added to some commercial beers and if you wish to produce a drink free from all adulterations then this additive may easily be omitted.

The third process in the conditioning is maturation and this is a collective term for all the processes that improve the quality of a beer with ageing. It is the result of the marrying together of existing flavours and chemical reactions which produce new ones. Maturation of beer is generally misunderstood, with periods of five to ten days often quoted. Beers are certainly drinkable in this time and I would encourage any beginner to try the brew then, but once you have been making beer for some time and begin to build up stocks (well that's the theory anyway) you can afford to wait for your beer to mature. Try the beer after various periods of time and decide for yourself whether you think that the extra storage period is worth it. Personally I prefer well-matured beers, but you will need a suitable place to store the beer, and far more bottles. When storing all beers, except lagers, keep them at 65–70°F (18–21°C). This will ensure that the beer is fully gassed. Most beers should then be stored as near to 45°F (7°C) as possible and lagers at just above freezing point. This is not always possible and few problems result from a higher temperature, but the life of any beer does decrease with increases in storage temperature. Don't worry too much about storage temperatures unless you plan to keep the beer for a long time or else live in a tropical region, when you should store the beer in the coolest part of the house. Storage times depend on the temperature, which causes the yeast deposit at the bottom of the bottle to decompose, and on the type of beer. High gravity beers with a high hopping rate are the slowest to mature and keep for the longest period.

Just because the maximum storage time has

FERMENTING AND FINISHING BEER

1. AFTER THREE OR FOUR DAYS REMOVE LID AND TAKE OFF MOST OF HEAD AND ALL BROWN GUM. STIR TO DISSOLVE AIR.

COVER: REPEAT 3 OR 4 DAYS LATER

2.

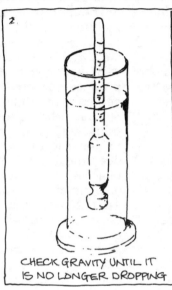

CHECK GRAVITY UNTIL IT IS NO LONGER DROPPING

3.

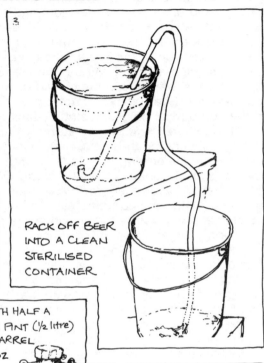

RACK OFF BEER INTO A CLEAN STERILISED CONTAINER

4. ADD HEADING LIQUID IF NECESSARY

IF DRY HOPPING KEEP A FURTHER 3 DAYS AND THEN STRAIN

5. EITHER BOTTLE, PRIMING WITH HALF A LEVEL TSP. PER PINT (½ litre) OR 4/5 FILL A BARREL PRIME WITH 2oz SUGAR PER GAL (50gm/litre)

6. ALLOW TO CONDITION AND SERVE.

been exceeded never throw any beer away until you have tested it. If it tastes good, it is good. Many commercial brewers pasteurise their beers by heating to about 150°F (65°C) but you should not attempt to pasteurise your own beers at home because at such high temperatures the bottles could explode.

One of the disadvantages of serving living beers from the bottle is that if you do not pour carefully, the yeast deposit may be transferred to the glass. This presents no problem if you discard the bottom inch of beer. Alternatively, you can decant the beer into a jug, before pouring into the glass. Always pour the beer into a well-washed glass, as the slightest trace of grease on the side of the glass can destroy the head of the drink.

There are occasions when the yeast deposit can be inconvenient—if you are having a party, or want to take the beer on a picnic. If you need a beer free of deposit then it can be removed by using 'Beerbrite' caps. These consist of a large plastic teat which during the early stage of conditioning takes the place of the traditional crown cap. The beer is inverted after two days and is kept at an angle of 45 degrees for at least four weeks. A suitable stand can be made out of a cardboard box. The bottle is then rotated to ensure that all the yeast is deposited in the teat, which can be wired at its base to prevent the yeast returning to the bottle. The beer is then ready for serving. Alternatively, you can store the beer in the refrigerator for three-quarters of an hour, remove the wired teat and cap and fit either a reusable beer stopper or crown cork. The caps are provided with full instructions.

Another method of ensuring that a yeast sediment does not spoil the beer is to stand it in the refrigerator for two hours before serving. Pour the cold beer quickly into another bottle

ensuring that no sediment is transferred and recap. Some beer will be wasted and there is inevitably a loss of gas, but you should be able to get six clear bottles from seven pints.

When the beer is in the refrigerator, the carbon dioxide above the liquid is more soluble in the cold liquid than it is at room temperature and a large quantity dissolves. When the beer is opened, and providing it is poured with the minimum amount of sediment disturbance into a jug (cooled by placing in the refrigerator), it can be transferred to a new bottle with a negligible loss of gas. Do not use this technique with beers you wish to store, as the combined effect of the loss of gas and the air entering the bottle will accelerate decomposition by oxidation.

Most beers are best served cool and it is a good idea to keep a supply in the refrigerator so that a bottle may be taken out when required. Some years ago it was very popular to serve mulled beers which were prepared by pouring the beer into a ceramic mug and placing a red hot poker into the drink. Not only does this raise the temperature of the beer but it disperses much of the gas. It is really only done with dark beers.

If a bottle is only half-empty it can be re-stoppered and kept in the refrigerator for up to two days.

Many people are reluctant to take home-made beer to a party, or even serve it themselves, because the bottles look uninviting. It is possible to buy labels very cheaply to give the appearance of bought beers or you can even get labels with your own name printed on them.

When you have emptied beer bottles wash them out while they are still wet, otherwise the yeast dries out and leaves a deposit on the bottom which can be extremely difficult to remove. If you forget and find a dry deposit in the bottle, soak it in hot water to which detergent has been added. Scraping with a probe, or shaking with a slurry of sand and water seem to be the only really effective methods. Yeast deposits on the side are easily removed with a bottle brush.

Draught Beers

Serving draught beers at home is no problem due to the availability of a wide variety of plastic barrels and carbon dioxide dispensers. What we cannot produce is a true keg beer, which is a filtered non-living beer. Fortunately, keg beer drinkers soon accept home-made draught beers as a very agreeable alternative. New designs of barrel continually appear and your choice will depend on how much you are prepared to pay. Barrels that are capable of withstanding pressures of up to 10–15 p.s.i. and possessing a standard gauge fitting at the top to take a carbon dioxide bottle, are the best. Unless you intend to serve draught beers only occasionally, you will need to have a second barrel in which a fresh batch of beer can be conditioning whilst you are drinking the first. The initial outlay is higher for draught than bottled beer and there are usually no savings on running costs. Carbon dioxide bottles have to be bought and these are quite expensive items, nevertheless when bar prices are taken into consideration the outlay is soon recovered. There are two definite advantages. Firstly, there is less work involved in cleaning, sterilising and priming one barrel compared with several bottles, although it is still imperative that they are thoroughly cleaned out after use. Before buying any barrel always check that there is adequate access for cleaning.

The second advantage is that draught beers reach their prime far quicker than bottled beers. Draught beers are at their best three weeks from the day the yeast was added, whereas bottled beers, although drinkable at this stage, usually require a further month's storage before they are at their best.

Theoretically any beer can be served draught, but the most likely types are bitter, mild, lager and possibly Irish stout. Your idea of a bitter may be more like the recipe for Indian pale or a light ale. If this is the case then simply make the beer in the normal way but condition it in the barrel. You are unlikely to want old ales in large quantities because they are so strong and it is therefore better to bottle them.

Draught beers, especially lights and lagers, must be stored at a low temperature (the lower the better) as soon as fermentation is completed if you are really to enjoy them. Much of their character comes from conditioning. Separate outbuildings can be inconvenient, especially on an evening when it is pouring with rain. Before buying a barrel consider carefully where it is going to be placed, and the temperature at which the conditioning after the final fermentation will occur. Be careful that this is not too low or you will risk stuck fermentation.

The more carbon dioxide that is dissolved in draught beers the higher the quality. The gas above the beer is partly wasted, but if you leave the bottled beer in the refrigerator for some time before it is required gas will redissolve in the liquid. Once the gas has left the liquid in draught beers the only way to make it redissolve, apart from increasing the pressure (a method which has its limitations), is to stand the barrel in a very cold area for a long time. It is far easier to keep the beer in a cool place from the start.

To make a draught beer, conduct the fermentation in the same way as for bottled beers and when the hydrometer shows no further drop in gravity, syphon the beer into the barrel. Conditioning fermentation will now occur in the barrel. For this to happen an airspace must be left so that at least part of the beer is always under a head of carbon dioxide gas. Do not be tempted to fill the barrel completely and fit an airlock). This will not only help the beer to reach a better condition, but it is important in the dispensation process. Only fill a barrel to 80% of its volume or even slightly less. Dissolve two ounces of sugar in the minimum amount of water for every gallon of beer (50 gm per 5 litre) and add whilst stirring. Maintain the temperature 60–65°F (15.5–18°C) for ten days. Lager should be maintained at 50–55°F (10–13°C).

It has been suggested that before putting the beer in the barrel the air should be purged from the system by dispensing a carbon dioxide bottle into the keg. While this excludes the air on which many spoilage yeasts depend, I have found that by maintaining sterile conditions throughout complications do not arise and I omit this treatment. Gas cylinders are expensive and I do not advise their over-use. Moreover, the air that dissolves in the liquid is beneficial in restarting the fermentation process as is the air dissolved during racking.

Whilst recommending the omission of this precaution I must stress once again the importance of maintaining absolutely sterile conditions in either wine- or beer-making. Bacterial attack in high oxygen conditions seems to be more complicated than was previously thought and some houses are more prone to it than others, possibly due to a high build-up of spores in the area. If you do encounter any problems of this sort, see if purging the barrel with carbon dioxide cures them.

An alternative method of conditioning beer which can save a few days is to allow some of the sugars in the wort to do the conditioning for you. When you have made a beer several times, and know what the finishing gravity is, then you can transfer the beer to the barrel when the gravity is .004 above the final gravity. If this fails to yield enough gas then extra can always be provided from the CO_2 bottle when the final fermentation is complete. Place the keg in position and leave the beer to settle for a day or two before pulling off the first pint. For those who want a really top quality draught beer, though, it is better to allow up to ten days for the conditioning after fermentation has ceased.

If the drink was clear when it was placed in the barrel the first pint should also be clear. Never bottle or keg any beer in the hope that it will clear later. If problems are encountered before kegging, then the yeast should be changed for future brews as long as it responds to gelatine treatment. If not, then it is the result of either starch or protein hazes (which only occur with mashed or half-mashed beers) and you should look to your mashing technique. Where a haze develops in the barrel this will be due to yeast sediment. If it has not cleared after a week unscrew the CO_2 bottle, insert a prepared gelatine solution and leave for two days. (For methods of avoiding drawing the yeast from the bottom of the barrel see under accessories). Barrels prepared in this way will keep for several months, the exact time depending upon the type of beer that has been made. Apart from the slight drop in the carbon dioxide level the beer is in many respects similar to keg.

Do not be tempted to avoid using a carbon dioxide dispenser. It may appear to be unnecessary as the first few pints will pour from the barrel without the addition of induced pressure, due to the pressure above the liquid created by the conditioning gas. As the volume of the liquid decreases the gas expands and the pressure drops substantially. When a volume equal to that above the liquid has been drawn off, the liquid will no longer come cleanly out of the tap. As it comes out the barrel it will take in an equal quantity of air to fill the vacuum that the liquid's departure has created. This results in a gurgling sound, and an agitation in the beer as the air passes through it. This agitation will stir up the yeast sediment at the bottom of the barrel giving a cloudy beer. Moreover, the pressure reduction of the conditioning carbon dioxide, coupled with the air, produces a flat insipid drink. The air is likely to bring with it micro-organisms that will infect the beer and ultimately turn it into vinegar. Unlike the air which enters when the beer is first placed in the barrel, any entering at this stage will not be counteracted by a blanket of carbon dioxide formed as a result of fermentation.

The old way of serving beer was to rely entirely on gravity feed; the plug was taken out of the barrel and the beer was drawn off through the tap. This resulted in a beer containing far less gas than most of the modern types. When kept correctly, beers served in this way were considered by many to be the finest of all.

This method is not applicable to the kitchen brewer for two reasons. Gravity dispensing results in air displacing the beer. The only way that it is possible to serve the beer without fear of contamination is to consume it all within two or three days. This is only likely to be possible if you are holding a party.

The second objection to the technique is that temperature is more important here than with conventionally barrelled beers. The only conditioning gas in the beer is that formed during the final stages of fermentation and to ensure that most of it remains in solution the fermentation must be conducted at the lowest temperature consistent with the process continuing. The actual temperature will depend upon the tolerance of the yeast strain and can only be found by trial and error. Even after fermentation has ceased, and the beer is standing at its serving point, no rise in temperature can be tolerated as this would cause the beer to lose its gas. The best beers served in this fashion required a cellar and it was once common practice to collect the beer in a jug rather than disturb the barrel. Clearly and regrettably all this is beyond the home brewer.

If you find it impossible to obtain a carbon dioxide cylinder, then the only way in which you can serve the beer is to half-fill the keg initially and double the conditioning sugar. Do not increase the conditioning sugar without decreasing the volume of beer as this might make the barrel burst through excess pressure. Where a safety valve is fitted this will 'blow' before there is any danger to the barrel and you can increase the sugar for conditioning up to four ounces per gallon (125 gm per 5 litres). This will decrease the amount of expensive gas you have to use. (There is nothing to be gained by exceeding this amount as it will only vent and be wasted).

It is possible to dispense beer without adding conditioning sugar by providing all the gas from the cylinder. This is done to save conditioning time. If the liquid is racked into the barrel it will be clear and the beer can be served as soon as the gas is turned on. Since no more fermentation can occur, there being no unfermented sugar, there are no problems with yeast sediment and the beer is clear to the last pint. This should be the case with all types of beer if they are correctly dispensed. This method is a little more expensive, but since it does result in less delay and less work the cost is probably justified. It is advisable to drive out the air from the barrel before adding the beer as fermentation is now complete and no carbon dioxide will be produced. Any air may oxidise the beer, especially the delicately flavoured types like lager.

Personally I feel that beers prepared in this way are not as well-conditioned as those made by fermentation in the barrel. When fermentation occurs in the liquid, minute quantities of gas are generated and in dissolving saturate the liquid by the time the conditioning fermentation is complete. When gas is applied above the liquid it takes time both to dissolve and replace the air that entered the liquid during racking. The beer may therefore be undergassed, until the system has had chance to reach equilibrium.

One method of dispensing beer that I do not like is from a sherry five. These are five gallon draught sherry containers which are filled with beer and the first few pints are discharged by the pressure of the conditioning gas. When this has been used up the sides of the pliable container are squeezed to increase the pressure and more liquid is discharged. Unless you are extremely careful the yeast sediment is disturbed. Another drawback is that they cannot withstand very high pressure and will probably explode if the priming sugar is too high. Sherry fives can be used initially as fermentation vessels to avoid expense, but even here they are not ideal since it is virtually impossible to skim the beer without cutting off the top.

Barrel Accessories

Wherever possible I have tried to suggest ways in which you might economise. However a good barrel will last for years and pay for itself many times. This is also true of the two accessories you should fit to your barrel. A pressure valve will avoid the risk of a blow-out which could prove extremely expensive, destroying the barrel and possibly damaging your room. The second accessory is the Sparklets Home Brew Tap which ensures that every pint you draw is clear and sometimes allows the beer to be drunk a few days earlier. It dispenses the beer by pressure from the top of the barrel. By drawing from the top of the liquid, which always clears first, you can be certain that even the final pints will be free of yeast sediment.

The carbon dioxide dispensing system is one which I have found to be virtually trouble-free but there are other systems available such as ones that trap the carbon dioxide from the primary fermentation and use this to dispense the beer. There are also a wide range of different barrels available. As the barrel will be with you for virtually the whole of your brewing career it is well worth studying what is available, either by visiting a home brew centre, or writing to the manufacturers for literature before buying.

Wooden Barrels

You may be tempted to serve your beer from a wooden barrel. My advice to you is forget it. You can obtain new barrels, perhaps even good secondhand ones, from a brewery, but after the first brew you are confronted with the problem of sterilisation. Commercial brewers usually sterilise their barrels with steam. High pressure cannot be produced in the kitchen, the only way of sterilising our barrels is with boiling water. Transporting and pouring boiling water is not a very safe operation. To sterilise a four and a half gallon barrel, you need to pour in at least eight pints (5 litres) of boiling water. With the holes plugged, roll the barrel to disperse the water evenly. When the water has cooled allow it to drain away. Such a method, whilst it will not guarantee absolute sterility, should be sufficient to allow you to use the container: bearing in mind the protection that conditioning fermentation will give. Under no circumstances attempt to sterilise the barrel with bleach. Apart from the strong smell of chlorine that escapes from the holes and which, if inhaled, can do considerable damage to health, the wood absorbs the bleach solution like a sponge and it is virtually impossible to wash it all out. The only way to remove the smell is to take out the bungs and allow the gas to gradually disperse. By the time this is complete the barrel will no longer be sterile.

Barrels, unless sterilised, will harbour vinegar-forming yeasts, and these may not be completely destroyed by mild sterilising agents such as Campden tablets. Their smell is not quite as strong as bleach but is equally objectionable and harmful.

Having sterilised the barrel, 80% fill it with beer and add dissolved priming sugar at the rate of two ounces per gallon (50 gm per 5 litres). Fit an airlock and bung in the hole in the barrel side. After five days remove the airlock and seal the hole. Stand the barrel on wooden mounts so that one end slopes slightly backwards to trap the yeast sediment at the base of the barrel furthest from the tap. Fit the tap, release the bung at the top of the beer, and serve the beer by gravity feed, covering the hole at the top with a damp cloth. This beer, relying on gravity feed, will only be at its best for a very short time.

The use of wooden barrels is extremely difficult for the amateur, and only the true enthusiast who is prepared for setbacks and disappointments before mastering the art should try them. If you have been given a beer barrel I suggest that you saw it in two and plant tulips in it!

With the exception of wooden barrels and filters for making keg beers, we can compete with the commercial brewer in all aspects of beer-making. We now have the ingredients and equipment, but above all the knowledge, that will soon become skill, to make top quality beers, brewed to our own individual palates at a fraction of the price that we would have to pay for them.

Chapter 9
Final Thoughts

Wine Circles

Perhaps the biggest disadvantage of home brewing is the lack of socialising that is associated with the activity. If you make your own beer you will be made welcome at most wine circles. In spite of their name, they usually have a section interested in home brewing, and members are usually only too willing to help beginners. Most circles usually run a programme of social events, including outings, picnics and parties where it is expected that you bring your own wines or beers.

Exhibiting Beers

With the increase in popularity of brewing, more and more small horticultural, as well as agricultural, shows have classes for home-made beer. Apart from the competition which is fun in itself, you can ask the judge his opinion of your beer and gain not only an assessment, but usually advice on any aspect of beer-making.

You do not need to make any special beers for showing: the beer that wins prizes must be clear, full-bodied with a balanced malty, hoppy taste and well-conditioned: the type of beer that you will normally be making and drinking.

Before entering a competition, study the schedule as far ahead of the show as possible. See if there are any special regulations in connection with the type of bottle that must be used, since failure to comply with these could result in disqualification.

If there are no special regulations, select a non-returnable bottle, ensure that there are no scratch marks on the sides, and wash the bottle thoroughly with warm water containing washing-up liquid. Fill the bottle to within half an inch to an inch (1.25–2.5 cm) of the top. Label according to the instructions given in the schedule.

Most people start making beer as an economy measure, but often it develops into an absorbing hobby in its own right.

Glossary of Brewing Terms

Alpha Acid Units (A.A.U.)
The quantity of acid responsible for the bitter taste in hops, expressed as percentage of the weight.

Acetic Acid
Acid responsible for the characteristic taste of vinegar. Occurs in brewing as a result of poor hygiene.

Adjuncts
Cereal-based ingredients other than malt incorporated in the mash.

Alcohol
Member of a group of organic chemicals formed in this production of beer. Generally used for one specific alcohol, ethanol (ethyl alcohol).

Amylase
Main action is to convert starch to sugar.

Attenuation
The conversion of sugars to alcohol during fermentation. Used to describe the drop in gravity during fermentation.

Bottom-Fermentation
Fermentation by lager yeasts, in which the majority of the yeast cells remains at the bottom of the fermentation vessel.

Burtonise
The process of adding epsom salts and gypsum to waters to imitate the brewing water of Burton-on-Trent.

Calcium Carbonate
Chemical name for chalk.

Calcium Sulphate
Chemical name for gypsum.

Campden Tablets
Sterilising agent, mainly sodium metabisulphite.

Carbohydrate
Class of chemical compounds including starch, sugar and cellulose.

Carbon Dioxide (CO_2)
A gas consisting of one part carbon and two parts oxygen released during fermentation.

Chalk
Common name for calcium carbonate.

Citric acid
Acid found in lemons.

Cold Break	The final precipitation of solids from the hopped wort, it occurs as a result of shock cooling.
Conditioning	The process of providing carbon dioxide to the finished beer.
Copper Finings	Finings, usually Irish moss, added during the boiling stage.
Decoction Mash	A system used in lager-brewing, in which the mash is conducted at different temperatures.
Dextrin	Carbohydrates, that are non- (or only slowly) fermentable.
Diastase	A name given to a mixture of alpha and beta amylase.
Diastase Active	Material, that through not having the diastase destroyed, is capable of converting cereal starches to sugars. Applied mainly to malt extracts.
Fermentation	The conversion of sugars to alcohol.
Fining	The process of adding finings.
Finings	Materials that aid clarification of beer.
Floating Mash Tun	Mash tun in which the grains are suspended to allow free passage of liquor.
Glucose	A sugar obtained from sucrose or starch by inversion.
Grist	Dry mixture of malts and adjuncts used in mashing.
Gravity (specific)	The weight of a liquid relative to an equal volume of water.
Gypsum	Common name for calcium sulphate.
Hardness of water	The reluctance of water to form a lather with soap. It is a measure of the concentration of certain calcium and magnesium salts in the liquid and is still used in the discussion of brewing water.
Hopping rate	The weight of hops that is added to a specified volume of wort.
Hot Break	The first part of the clarification process; it occurs when the wort is boiled with hops.
Hydrometer	An instrument for determining gravities.
Initial Fermentation	The stage at which the yeast breeds. Also termed primary fermentation.
Irish moss	Finings added prior to the end of the boiling.

Isinglass	The best of all finings, for final clarification—difficult for the amateur to use.
Lactic Acid	A mild acid, ideal for using in brewing.
Lactose	Milk sugar—being virtually unfermentable it is ideal for sweetening stouts and brown ales.
Liquor	Term used by professional brewers to describe the water used for making beer.
Malt	Roasted, germinated barley grains.
Malt Extract	The products of the mash tun, evaporated to a semi-liquid or solid state
Mashing	The process of extraction of sugars, and the conversion of starch to sugars in malt.
Mash Tun	Vessel in which mashing is conducted.
Maltose	Main fermentable sugar obtained from malted grains.
Maturation	The ageing of the beer.
Permanent Hardness	Hardness of water that cannot be removed by boiling.
pH	Method for expressing the acidity of alkalinity of a solution.
Priming	Providing the sugar necessary for the production of the conditioning carbon dioxide.
Priming Sugar	The sugar used for priming.
Proteins	Nitrogen-containing compounds, excess of which cause hazes in beers.
Racking	The process of separating the fermented beer from the yeast cells at the bottom of the fermenting vessel.
Rousing	Stirring during the initial fermentation to allow carbon dioxide to escape and to replace it in the liquid.
Sodium Chloride	Chemical name for table salt.
Sparging	Washing of mashed grains to ensure complete extraction of the sugars.
Starch	A non-fermentable carbohydrate.
Temporary Hardness	Hardness that can be removed by boiling.
Top-Fermentation	Fermentation in which the majority of the yeast rises to the top of the liquid during the initial ferment. Responsible for the production of most beers other than lagers.

Tincture of Iodine	A solution used to test for the presence of starch in mashing liquor.
Wort	The sugar-rich solution obtained by mashing the grains.
Yeast	Simple plant that converts certain sugars to alcohol.

Suppliers

Home beer-making supplies may be obtained in the United Kingdom from home brew shops, multiple chemists and a variety of other outlets. Overseas supplies can be purchased by post from firms which advertise a mail order service.

Specialist Equipment
The following firms market specialised items mentioned in the text, and would be pleased to advise you of your nearest stockists or mail direct to any part of the world.

'Bruheat Buckets' Ritchie Products
Rolleston Road
Burton-on-Trent
Staffs
England

'BeerBrite' Caps Southern Vineyards
Hove
Sussex

'Sparklets' Beer Barrels and Dispensing Systems Sparklets International
Queen Street
London N17 8J4

The Do's and Don'ts of Homebrewing

Do — Ensure that all equipment is clean and sterilised, wild yeast can render beers undrinkable.

Do — Experiment, adjust recipes to suit your palate and techniques to suit your convenience. However, only adjust one factor with each brew so that you can measure the effect accurately.

Do — Read the relevant theory before attempting to deviate in any way from the standard procedures. This ensures that you will not have an expensive failure.

Do — Keep a record, so that you can refer back to your previous brews in the future.

Do — Make kits up to the manufacturer's instructions before deciding to adjust them to your palate.

Do — Try the different kits on the market before deciding which one you prefer.

Do Not — Listen to those people who tell you that it is not possible to make a decent beer from kits.

Do Not — Economise with malt and other ingredients, the cost of these are only a fraction of the price of beer.

Do Not — Be deterred because you cannot obtain the exact variety of hops. Until such time as you can, use the best that are available.

Do Not — Be careless about storing hops, dried malt, and crushed malt. They always keep better in an air-tight container.

Do Not — Be frightened to discuss any points, such as the local water with your home brew supplier. He will have knowledge of local conditions.

Do Not — Add sugar just to increase the alcohol. This will give you, in addition to a headache, a strong beer with very little character.

Index

Making Your Own Paté

Joyce Van Doorn

Pâté is a savoury mixture of meat, poultry, pulses or fish, sometimes covered with a pastry crust. This book mostly consists of mouth-watering recipes from around the world including dishes not normally described as pâtés in Great Britain such as terrines, mousses, gallantines, rillets, pies and flans.

Author

Joyce van Doorn is a lecturer, writer and broadcaster.

8″ x 8″, 120 pages
Full colour photographic cover
25 line drawings
ISBN 0 907061 01 X   Hardback £5.95
ISBN 0 907061 02 8   Paperback £2.95

Making Your Own Preserves

Jane & Rob Avery

A comprehensive book of over 150 recipes with careful instructions and all the essential background.

Contents

1   Methods, Advantages and Scope
2   General Principles
3   Equipment and Materials
4   Bottling
5   Conserves and Syrups
6   Jams and Jellies
7   Curds, Cheeses and Butters
8   Marmalades, Mincemeats and Crystalized Fruits
9   Pickles and Chutneys
10 Sauces, Vegetable Juices and Vinegars
11 Salting and Drying
12 Meat, Fish and Shellfish

Authors

Rob and Jane Avery are freelance writers specialising in fishing, self-sufficiency and cookery topics.

8" x 8", 120 pages
Full colour photographic cover
Numerous line drawings
ISBN 0 907061 17 6   Hardback £6.95
ISBN 0 907061 18 4   Paperback £2.95

The Bread Book

Debbie Boater

A very basic book with fundamental information about the important role that bread plays in our diet and how to make it in its original, nutritious, wholesome form. A wide variety of recipes are included which cover breads, savoury breads, sweet breads, flat breads, pancakes, muffins and pastries.

Author

Debbie Boater is a teacher and founder of the Wholefood School of Nutrition.

8" x 8", 96 pages
Full photographic cover
25 line drawings
ISBN 0 904727 95 5   Hardback £5.95
ISBN 0 904727 96 3   Paperback £2.95

Bean Cuisine

Janet Horsley

Bean Cuisine is a comprehensive guide to the cooking of beans and pulses, useful both as a reference book and as a recipe book.

An introductory chapter traces the historic, economic and nutritional aspects of bean cooking, and explains how to use them to make well balanced, nutritious meals. An illustrated A-Z is included to aid recognition, as well as all the information needed to prepare, cook, freeze and sprout the beans.

Author

Janet Horsley is a cookery and nutrition lecturer.

8" x 8" 96 pages
Illustrated with line drawings
Full colour photographic cover
ISBN 0 907061 32 X   Hardback £6.95
ISBN 0 907061 33 8   Paperback £2.95

Making Your Own Liqueurs

Joyce van Doorn

With the help of some simple equipment: a set of scales, glassware, a filter and a mixture of herbs, spices, flowers, fruits, sugar and alcohol, you can make your own liqueurs which will be as exotic and tasty as the commercial varieties. Over 200 different recipes are listed ranging from fruits in alcohol, ratafias, herb and flower liqueurs, to bitters and elixirs.

Author

Joyce van Doorn is a lecturer, writer and broadcaster.

8″ x 8″, 120 pages
Full colour photographic cover
65 line drawings
ISBN 0 907061 03 6   Hardback £5.95
ISBN 0 907061 04 4   Paperback £2.95

Tea

Eelco Hesse

Tea drinking originated in China and Japan more than 2000 years ago. This book recounts the fascinating history of tea drinking and the colourful development of the Tea Trade over the centuries.

The author also examines the tools of tea making and how tea is grown and processed throughout the world. There is a section on tea blending and full instructions on making a 'perfect cup of tea'. The appendices contain anecdotes, songs and poetry about tea as well as useful addresses for further information and obtaining supplies.

Author

Eelco Hesse is a well-known authority on tea and the tea trade.

8″ x 8″, 120 pages
Full colour photographic cover
Numerous line drawings and engravings
ISBN 0 907061 05 2   Hardback £6.95
ISBN 0 907061 06 0   Paperback £2.95

Winemaking Month by Month

Brian Leverett

"If you enjoy making wines as well as drinking them you wil find this book both informative and enjoyable. It gives recipes for each month, according to what is in season as well as general guidance on home brewing"
Birmingham Post
"Useful, readable and logically presented."
Do-It-Yourself Magazine

Author

Brian Leverett is a lecturer, journalist and broadcaster.

8″ x 8″, 120 pages
Full colour photographic cover
37 line drawings and tables
ISBN 0 904727 93 9   Hardback £5.95
ISBN 0 904727 94 7   Paperback £2.95

Home Beermaking

Brian Leverett

This book is more than just a collection of recipes with instructions. It explains clearly, with straightforward diagrams, the complex brewing process and how to achieve the best possible results at home, whether from a can or with the traditional ingredients. The unique fault finder chart will help you overcome many of the problems that you may have had with previous attempts at home brewing.

Author

Brian Leverett is a lecturer, journalist and broadcaster.

8" X 8", 120 pages
Full colour photographic cover
32 line drawings and tables
ISBN 0 907061 07 9 Hardback £5.95
ISBN 0 907061 08 7   Paperback £2.95